CITIZEN SWAIN

To Andy:

Hooray for Us

AA UW.

Best,

[signature]

CITIZEN SWAIN

TALES FROM A MINNESOTA LIFE

★ ★ ★

TOM H. SWAIN

WITH LORI STURDEVANT

*To Judy –
with appreciation
Lori Sturdevant*

University of Minnesota Press

Minneapolis

London

The Hubert H. Humphrey School of Public Affairs at the University of Minnesota is honored to recognize the outstanding civic contributions of Tom Swain with the Thomas H. Swain Fellowship in Public Leadership in the Mid-career Master of Public Affairs program. It is awarded to exceptional mid-career professionals annually in support of their graduate studies. Sales of this book will contribute to the fellowship.

The photograph of Judy Garland is by Marty Nordstrom / *Minneapolis Tribune*; reprinted courtesy of the *Minneapolis–St. Paul Star Tribune*. The photograph of Elmer L. Andersen during his gubernatorial campaign is reprinted courtesy of the Minnesota Historical Society. All other photographs are courtesy of the author.

Published by the University of Minnesota Press
111 Third Avenue South, Suite 290
Minneapolis, MN 55401–2520
http://www.upress.umn.edu

LIBRARY OF CONGRESS CATALOGING-IN-PUBLICATION DATA
Swain, Tom H.
Citizen Swain: tales from a Minnesota life / Tom H. Swain with Lori Sturdevant.
ISBN 978-0-8166-9461-7 (hc)
1. Swain, Tom H. 2. Minnesota—History. 3. Minnesota—Politics and government. 4. Minnesota—Social conditions. I. Title.
F610.3.S84A3 2015
977.6—dc23   2014046650

Printed in the United States of America on acid-free paper

The University of Minnesota is an equal-opportunity educator and employer.

21   20   19   18   17   16   15   9   8   7   6   5   4   3   2   1

For Arlene
1922–2015

The University of Minnesota Press gratefully acknowledges the generous assistance provided for the publication of this book by the following institutions and individuals.

The Honorable Richard B. Beeson Jr. and Mary Don E. Beeson

Robert J. Burgett

Charles M. Denny Jr.

Mark C. and Catherine N. Dienhart

Jo Anne M. Driscoll

L. Steven and Mary Goldstein

Karen L. Himle

Eric W. and Karen F. Kaler

The Honorable David M. and Janis Larson

Catherine A. Lawrence and Lee E. Sheehy

Peggy and David Lucas

Elizabeth A. Malkerson

Joel D. and Lois A. Maturi

The David and Linda Mona Fund of the Minneapolis Foundation

Steven and Marilyn Rothschild

Kathleen M. Schmidlkofer

Barbara J. Swain

Thomas M. and Laura C. Swain

The Travelers Companies, Inc.

Contents

A Life of Service

Lori Sturdevant

"TOM SWAIN IS LIKE HUR." That's what one of Minnesota's Lutheran leaders, the Reverend David Preus, said when I told him that I was compiling the many stories Tom Swain often tells about his long life and work in Minnesota public affairs.

"Tom is like her?" I responded quizzically. What long-serving, story-telling Minnesota woman did he have in mind?

"No, Hur—H-u-r," the good cleric clarified. Preus related the story from Exodus 17 of the great battle between the ancient Israelites and the Amalekites. Moses, his brother Aaron, and his chief of staff / executive vice president / senior adviser Hur climbed a hill to watch the battle. The trio discovered that whenever Moses extended his hands and arms, Israelite forces appeared to be gaining ground. When he dropped his arms, the battle turned in the Amalekites' favor.

Don't drop those arms, Hur advised. He and Aaron found a stone on which their governor/CEO/president could sit. To their relief, sitting evidently did not alter the phenomenon. But those old arms could not fall, they concluded, or General Joshua and his soldiers in the valley below would be in trouble. So brother Aaron stood on one side of Moses, and Hur on the other. They held up his hands all day, until darkness fell. "So Joshua overcame Amalek," verse 13 reports.

I like to think that verse's matter-of-fact announcement reflects the matter-of-fact manner of Hur/Swain. He's the guy who one day is upholding his leader to win the battle. The next day, he's raising money for the library or new police gear, or planning a civic celebration, or promoting better jobs, or getting his town out of debt, or recruiting conventions or businesses or candidates for government offices.

Tom Swain has performed crucial service to his community. He kept vital institutions functioning so that others could have the luxury of taking those institutions for granted. He spotted ways to make things better, sold others on his ideas, then carried out the plan with orderly efficiency.

Such public servants often labor out of the limelight, with little public recognition. Hur is remembered because he had a high-level agent who said, in essence, "This ought to be told in a book." Verse 14 reports: "Then the Lord said to Moses, 'Write this on a scroll as something to be remembered.'"

For years, Tom's friends have told him that his experiences are "something to be remembered," not just recounted for a laugh at social gatherings, which is how I first heard many of them. Tom's stories are rich oral history, of the sort future scholars will prize. They contain nuggets of insight that explain how today's Minnesota came into being. They are loaded with inspiration, reflecting the can-do attitude and sense of stewardship that Tom and his generational peers brought home from World War II. They are a road map to the active citizenship that the most powerful democracy in world history needs. They are also entertaining. Tom is an excellent storyteller who brings out the humanity in the people he describes, including himself. He joyfully recounts their successes and gently describes their foibles in ways respectful to all.

Tom's friends and family urged him to write a memoir and asked me to be his writing partner. I didn't need much persuasion. I knew Tom slightly for many years before I came to know him well in 1996. I was the *Star Tribune* editorial writer assigned to cover the University of Minnesota, and he was the new vice president for institutional relations, a job that included funneling information to journalists like me. Tom did me a great turn two years later when he recruited me to help his dear friend, former governor Elmer L. Andersen, write his autobiography. *A Man's Reach*, published by the University of Minnesota Press in 2000, was an early fruit of our long friendship. This book is another.

* * *

TOM AND I OWE THANKS to many people for contributions to this project. Our spark plug was Peggy Lucas, a cofounder of Brighton Development Corporation and a member of the University of Minnesota Board of Regents. We consider ourselves fortunate to be in Peggy's orbit. Her persistent persuasion and unflagging enthusiasm convinced us to stop merely talking about a book and start writing one.

Peggy helped convince others to provide the financial support this project required, and she and her husband, David, donated generously. We are grateful to Tom's longtime employer The Travelers Companies, Inc., and his friends and fans Richard and Mary Don Beeson, Robert Burgett, Charles M. Denny Jr., Mark and Catherine Dienhart, Karen Himle, Eric and Karen Kaler, David and Janis Larson, Catherine Lawrence and Lee Sheehy, Elizabeth Malkerson, Joel and Lois Maturi, David and Linda Mona, Steven and Marilyn Rothschild, and Kathleen Schmidlkofer.

Tom's son-in-law Steve Goldstein initially approached me with the idea for *Citizen Swain*. Steve possesses great energy and optimism, and he has done much in the service of the Twin Cities and the University of Minnesota. He would surely say that he has simply followed his father-in-law's example.

When we got serious, other members of both of our families pitched in to help. Tom's four children, Jo Anne Driscoll, Barbara Swain, Mary Goldstein, and Tom M. Swain, were ever ready to find a missing name, date, or memory. Each of them also contributed financially to this project. The photo archives of the Swain family provided the photographs in this book, unless otherwise credited. Thanks to Bruce Bjerva of the *Star Tribune* for unearthing the photograph of Judy Garland and John Foster Dulles from the newspaper's archives. My husband, Martin Vos—a Swain fan in his own right—was an excellent copy editor, as he has been on all of my books. I am grateful for his acceptance of the nights, weekends, and vacation days these ventures consume.

I am grateful to my employer, the *Star Tribune*, for allowing me time away from daily duties to complete *Citizen Swain*, the ninth book about notable Minnesotans I have worked on as author or editor.

Tom has a prodigious memory, but occasionally it was supplemented by conversations with admired friends and colleagues. We were happy to have help from Howard Guthmann, Ruby Hunt, Kathy Yaeger, Michael Scandrett, and Patricia Johnson.

I regret that Arlene Swain could no longer help us remember events and experiences. Her memory has been damaged by strokes and vascular dementia, but her loving, laughing, guiding spirit has infused Tom's life for nearly seventy years and is inseparable from his story. She appears again and again on the pages that follow, sometimes explicitly, sometimes as an unnamed but ever-present force in Tom's life, nudging him to be his best self in service to others. It is entirely fitting that this book is dedicated to her.

CHAPTER I

"Miss Pep"

MINNEAPOLITANS LOVE TO SING. One could say that I owe my existence to that fact. My mother would never have come to Minneapolis or met my father were it otherwise.

Marion Lucille Holliday was born on June 22, 1894, and was called Lucille or Lucy so exclusively that I was not aware her first name was Marion until I was grown. She was raised in comfort as a doctor's daughter in Traverse City, Michigan, until her father, Dr. Albert Holliday, died when she was twelve. In addition to his only daughter, he left a widow, Charlotte Shaw Holliday, and two sons, Lewis, a future newspaperman, and Tom, who suffered from a malady that caused him to be institutionalized and to die young. I am named for him.

Dr. Holliday also left his family in weakened financial condition, as often happened when breadwinners died too soon before Social Security became law. Lucy loved music and might have studied it seriously even if her father had lived. With him gone, she couldn't afford to just dabble. She enrolled in the Detroit Conservatory of Music and Thomas Normal School in Detroit and was certified as a music teacher. Her quest for a good-paying job (and probably for a little adventure, too) took her to Fargo, North Dakota, for a year, then to Crookston, Minnesota, and the Northwest School of Agriculture. It was a residential high school, created in 1906 for farm kids in a part of the state where high schools were few and far between. Eventually, it became the University of Minnesota Crookston. My mother was hired there in 1917, soon after the nation entered World War I. It may be that a war-induced labor shortage gave her a chance at employment that otherwise would have gone to a man, foreshadowing what millions of American women experienced during World War II. I recently received a yearbook from

1917–18 at Northwest. She is smiling happily on every page related to music, but it had to be tough for her to be a newcomer in such a sparsely populated place, especially while all the young men her age were in uniform somewhere far away.

One night a scheduled speaker who had attracted a crowd from the community as well as the school was late in arriving. Miss Holliday was pressed into service to lead the audience in singing until the speaker arrived. It was her first experience with that kind of impromptu song leading. I don't know if my mother had ever been a sports cheerleader. But she combined a cheerleader's methods with those of a choir director to rev up that crowd. She enjoyed it, and so did the audience. In the days that followed, she used the same pep-rally techniques with her students and found that they produced a better result than merely standing and waving a baton.

The war ended on November 11, 1918, but in Minneapolis, the War Camp Community Service continued to operate. A precursor of the USO, it provided a variety of services to soldiers coming and going from deployments in Europe. In December 1918, it advertised that it wanted to hire a song leader to entertain the troops. A *Minneapolis Sunday Journal* article dated June 8, 1919, describes what happened next: "She jumped on a train, came to Minneapolis and has been making Minneapolis sing ever since."

The banner headline places my mother's work in the context of Prohibition, which was on its way to ratification as an amendment to the U.S. Constitution in the summer of 1919. It reads, "Jazz—It's Taken J. Barleycorn's Place," and sits atop seven—seven!—photos of vivacious Lucille Holliday in action as a song leader. She pranced, grinned, cajoled, pointed, jumped, yelled, and evidently put on quite a show. Her repertoire consisted of the popular hits of World War I, songs like "Pack Up Your Troubles," "Smiles," and "Ja-Da." That was what passed for jazz in Minneapolis in 1919. "She was Billy Sunday put to music," the article says. A subheadline read, "Lots of Pep." Soon, and for a long time thereafter, Lucy Holliday would be "Miss Pep" in Minneapolis.

The songfest described in that article was the welcome home party at the University of Minnesota for the 151st Field Artillery. It was Minnesota's contribution to the Rainbow Division that was created from the National Guard units of twenty-six states at the start of the war. It was also my dad's outfit.

I'd like to be able to claim that my parents met the night of the party that made the big splash in the *Sunday Journal*. Or that they were romantically thrown together a few months earlier as part of a Minnesota delegation that went to the founding meeting of the American Legion in St. Louis on May 8–10, 1919. They were both there, and the Minnesotans succeeded in landing the first American Legion national convention in Minneapolis the following November.

But their actual meeting didn't happen until September 1919 at the Minneapolis Army and Navy Club—or so stated the *Minneapolis Journal* report on their engagement a few months later. It was news that 151st Field Artillery 2nd Lt. Earl Swain and the young woman who "has sung in virtually every organization in Minneapolis" were to be married. Lucy Holliday was described as the "supervisor of entertainment" for the club at which they met. Her photograph was included with the article; his wasn't. From the outset, it was clear who was the celebrity in the family.

Earl Edmond Swain was born on April 30, 1896, in Minneapolis. Though the state was not yet forty years old, he already represented the fourth generation of Swains in Minnesota. My great-great-grandfather Nehemiah Swain homesteaded on Union Lake, about fifteen miles west of Northfield, in 1856, two years before statehood. His neighbors were a family named Humphrey; one of the Swain girls married a Humphrey. When my grandmother died shortly after World War II, I was startled at her funeral when Mayor Hubert Humphrey sat down next to me. When I looked at him quizzically, he said, "We're related." I learned that day that Humphrey and I were distant cousins—second cousins once removed, to be precise.

Nehemiah was born in Massachusetts from a line of Swains that arrived from Britain in the middle of the seventeenth century and helped found the English settlement on Nantucket Island. He was a teacher and minister before coming to Minnesota as a homesteader. How long the Swains farmed at Union Lake isn't clear to me, but Nehemiah didn't make a success of it. Later he was a dentist and no more successful at that than at farming. His widow died in the county poor farm.

A well-remembered family story had nothing to do with crops or livestock. One afternoon in early September 1876, the surviving remnants of the Jesse James gang showed up at the farm seeking a place to spend the night. Unbeknownst to Nehemiah, they were on the lam after their botched attempt to rob the Northfield Bank. Nehemiah offered them his barn. When he checked the barn the next morning, his guests were gone, but a $20 gold piece was left behind—a precious sum in those days.

The family's farming venture ended in about 1885 when my great-grandfather Howard founded a hardware store in Minneapolis, H. L. Swain & Co. It was originally on East Hennepin Avenue, a main commercial street in the oldest part of the city, independently incorporated as St. Anthony until 1872. In about 1890, the store moved to 413 Fourteenth Avenue SE, in what is now the Dinkytown commercial district near the University of Minnesota campus. By then, it was selling coal and firewood as well as hardware, and not long after that, the hardware line was sold to William Simms. He made Simms Hardware a Dinkytown fixture for years. My grandfather, Charles L. Swain, took over the business in 1898, moved it to 408 Fourteenth Avenue, acquired a partner named Farmer, and expanded by adding a hauling service. Among its specialties was hauling the trunks of arriving university students to their dorms and apartments, and back to the train station again at semester's end. The company's wagons and horses—and eventually trucks—were housed between Fourteenth and Fifteenth Avenues on the site now occupied by the Dinkytown McDonald's.

When he came home from France in 1919, Dad returned to the Swain Farmer Fuel and Transfer Co., by then at 423 Fourteenth Avenue SE. He spent one year at the university before the war, but after military service his studies were over. In the 151st he'd been a sergeant who saw enough action to be gassed, sustain a concussion, and receive a battlefield promotion, which happens when the officer in an outfit is injured or killed. He didn't talk much about any of that, but it was bound to have lasting effects. Nor did he say much about his mother, Mabel Daugherty Swain, who died when he was a small boy soon after giving birth to his younger sister, also named Mabel. My grandfather then married a woman named Julie, who pretty much lived up to the reputation stepmothers have in children's stories. That union gave my dad two younger half-brothers, Bill and Ray. Bill's widow, Astrid, a native of Sweden, is my contemporary, still living in Minneapolis. I'm one of the few fellows in his nineties who continues to have lunch dates with his aunt.

Mother and Dad were married on August 17, 1920, in her mother's backyard in Traverse City. The ceremony was described in rich detail in the Traverse City newspaper. Mother saved that clipping, and she underlined only one sentence: "She is accomplished musically and has gained the distinction of being the only woman community song leader selected by any state, and has served in that capacity in Minneapolis for the past two years."

The young couple set up housekeeping at an upstairs duplex at 1105 Sixth Street SE. It was near First Congregational Church, where Mother directed a choir. I was born on July 4, 1921, at nearby St. Andrew's Hospital. I'm told that I arrived on a day that was hotter than heck, and I made things more difficult for my mother by checking in at a hefty nine pounds. Mother's celebrity put my birth into the newspaper. "What could possibly be more appropriate than that Mrs. Earl E. Swain, who before her marriage was Miss Lucille Holliday, should have a son born on the Fourth of July?" said the article Mother saved from the *Minneapolis Argus,* a weekly newspaper that served the city's east side. That story said my name was Thomas Jackson Swain—and it wasn't wrong. That was the name on my birth certificate. But I was always told my name was Thomas Holliday Swain, the name that Mother evidently preferred. When I needed a passport as an adult, it was a hassle to prove that Thomas Holliday Swain and Thomas Jackson Swain were the same person.

Mother's original Minneapolis job had evolved into a position with the city's Park and Recreation Board, which hosted community songfests in city parks on summer nights from 1919 until about 1950. These weren't little neighborhood parties. On pleasant evenings they drew upwards of 30,000 people. I'm sure Mother's pep contributed to their popularity. "Within a week" of taking that job, "she had the whole town singing," the *Minneapolis Tribune* said in another article about my birth.

Mother gave up that job when I was born "and has been singing lullabies instead of stirring war melodies" since, said a *Minneapolis Journal* article in 1924. It reported that she was coming out of her self-imposed maternity leave to lead songs at a fund-raising event for the Minneapolis Civic and Commerce Association, a forerunner of today's United Way. A photo of Mother feeding my one-year-old brother Bob in a high chair, with three-year-old me standing by, accompanied the story. It was my newspaper photo debut.

My twin brothers Joe and Jerry were born in 1926, and our family moved to a house at the city's outskirts, 5215 Clinton Avenue S., near what was then Pearl Swamp and is now Pearl Park. Our house backed up to the swamp. It was a place of wild wonder, where muskrats and raccoons lived and a band of neighbor boys could play imaginative games for hours unimpeded by adult supervision. A kid could get hurt there, too, and I did a few times. I fractured my ankle in one incident and my collarbone in another. There was no such thing as municipal garbage service then. People burned their trash out back. I wasn't very old when I was left in charge of one fire that got out of hand and spread into the swamp. I was in trouble then!

It wasn't long before "Miss Pep" was back in demand and in action. When the Minneapolis Auditorium opened on June 4, 1927, she led a five-hundred-voice chorus at the dedication ceremony. She was soon directing a number of choirs, among them the Pillsbury Pipers, a choral group at Pillsbury Settlement House; the YWCA Chorus; the children's choir at Plymouth Congregational Church; and for a run of at least nine holiday seasons, the Christmas Chorus that performed at Dayton's Department Store's auditorium. For many years, she also played the viola in the Minneapolis Civic Orchestra, which was a step below the Minneapolis Symphony Orchestra (today's Minnesota Orchestra). When there was a charity benefit that needed a musical leader or a viola player, she was often called. Her scrapbook of newspaper clippings indicates that she found a lot of satisfaction in her musical career.

As a kid, I don't think I was aware of how well known and popular

Mother was. I did know that she was in charge at home. She wasn't a softie. She had a strong sense of self-discipline, and she was a big believer in instilling responsibility and good conduct in her sons. She was keen for me to get an after-school job as soon as I was old enough to work. I sold magazines—*Saturday Evening Post, Ladies Home Journal, Country Gentleman*—starting at about age ten.

Then at age eleven or twelve, I got my first paper route delivering the *Minneapolis Evening Journal*. My first route was from Fifty-Fourth Street to Sixty-Second Street north to south, and Chicago Avenue to Cedar Avenue east to west. That was a big territory for a kid on a bike in the winter, and it was sparsely populated. I only had 32 customers, so I didn't make much money. Later I got a smaller, more densely populated route farther north, with 120 customers. I was making pretty good money then. But one bitterly cold day I put my head down, pumped like blazes, and ran into the back end of the Shenandoah Pharmacy delivery truck. The front end of my bike crumpled. I wasn't badly hurt, but getting that bike fixed pinched my income pretty hard. That happened during the awful winter of 1936, which was followed by a brutally hot summer. One day that summer I became so dizzy at the corner of Forty-Ninth Street and Elliot Avenue that I had to stop and sit on the grass. A woman took pity on me and brought me a glass of water that refreshed me enough that I could finish my route.

Dad was usually tired when he came home and would often flop down on the couch rather than doing things around the house or with us boys. Mother wasn't our playmate either. But she kept track of us and insisted on good behavior. She tried, unsuccessfully I'm afraid, to interest me in music. I took piano lessons for a while and had the lead in an operetta in junior high school before my voice changed. But she eventually gave up on any hope that I'd follow her into music.

I was more aware of Dad's connections. His Dinkytown business, Swain Farmer Fuel and Transfer, was small. It might have owned four or five delivery trucks. But he was evidently highly regarded by others in the trucking business, so much so that in the midst of the bloody 1934 Teamsters Strike, a group of smaller employers asked Dad to serve as their negotiator during federal mediation with the union in hopes of hastening an end to hostilities that were crippling the city's economy and sorely dividing its citizenry. Dad may have been chosen in part because he had served in World War I with the Dunne brothers, Vincent, Miles, and Grant, who were Teamsters Union leaders. In addition, my dad's half-brother Bill was a member of Teamsters Local 574 (later 544).

That made us typical of many Minneapolis families that summer. We had connections to both warring camps in the protracted dispute. I was too young to fully appreciate the tense situation that had developed in the warehouse district, though I heard plenty of inflated talk about the union being loaded with communists who were trying to turn Minneapolis into a Soviet-style state. Employers and their police allies employed shotguns to try to break the strike and the union, and the union members fought back with bricks and clubs. Four people died and scores were wounded in several violent outbreaks. One of our neighbors was among those who sustained a head injury. I'm not quite sure what Dad did as a negotiator, but the strike ended in a way that restored peace and tilted power in labor's direction in Minneapolis in a lasting way.

One of Dad's friends during World War I was Bernie Bierman, a Litchfield, Minnesota, native who was a University of Minnesota football star before joining the Marines. He became a coach, and after stints in Montana, Mississippi, and Louisiana, he returned as head coach of the Golden Gophers in 1932. With Dad's business so close to campus, Bierman and Dad quickly renewed their friendship. Dad was also a friend of athletic director Frank McCormick. In those years before big athletic scholarships, coaches often helped their players find jobs in the community in the off-season. Dad contributed to Bierman's program by employing some of his players and helping others make connections with other potential employers near campus.

When Bierman returned, I was eleven and in love with Gopher football, as were most of my friends. Minnesota had no major league professional sports teams then, so we avidly followed the Gophers. The whole family did, including Mom. When I was about thirteen or fourteen, Dad arranged for some Gopher players to come to my birthday party. I remember Vernal "Babe" LeVoir, Francis "Pug"

Lund, Bill Bevan, Stan Kostka, George Roscoe—names that might not mean much today, but they were heroes in my eyes and those of my buddies. It was a big thrill, one of the biggest of my childhood.

Dad's relationship with Bierman made a difference for me again after I graduated from Washburn High School in 1938 and enrolled at the University of Minnesota. Dad's business struggled during the Depression. A large coal company had moved in, and during the coldest winter in Minneapolis history—1936—it tried to squeeze small operators like Swain Farmer out of business by undercutting their price. Dad was forced to sell coal at a loss to compete. I remember him praying that the weather would warm up so he wouldn't lose money on every load of coal the firm sold. He hung on, but in the fall of 1938 it was clear that if I was going to enroll at the university, I would have to pay my own way. Dad did help in one way: he spoke to McCormick on my behalf. I got a job in the athletic ticket office, working for ticket manager Les Schroeder. Among my duties that first year was to operate the telephone switchboard during night basketball games. I was paid thirty-five cents an hour, missed every game—and considered myself fortunate.

Our family's life took a tragic turn in April 1939. As a sideline, Dad had started selling reflective materials for highway use. He had scheduled a sales trip to Madison, Wisconsin, to meet with that state's highway department. I dropped him off one morning at the Milwaukee Depot to catch the noon Hiawatha train to Madison. It was all very routine. His mood, the events of that morning and the days preceding it, and our parting were all unremarkable. None of us ever saw him or heard from him again. He disappeared from our lives that day, leaving an aching void and a huge mystery. After years of searching, asking, and wondering, I still don't know what happened to my dad.

As I reflect on those trying days now, I marvel at my mother's courage and self-control. If there were tears, they were private ones. With my brothers and me, she was strong, calm, and reassuring. We would be fine, and we would keep doing what we were supposed to do, she said. There was never a suggestion that, as the eldest, I ought to leave school and support the family. She wanted her sons to be educated. When hope that Dad would return was no longer realistic, she faced the reality that we had lost the house. At age forty-five, she needed work that paid more than her music career did. She found a three-bedroom apartment for the five of us at 4525 Nicollet Avenue. It had the virtues of being on a streetcar line and close to Washburn High School, where my brothers were students. And she found a job, first in a real estate office, then a year or two later selling life insurance for State Mutual Insurance Co. of Worcester, Massachusetts.

She did well and kept at it for nearly thirty years, channeling the same energy and discipline she displayed as a song leader into her sales work. For many years, I'd meet people who would tell me that my mother sold them an insurance policy. She joined the Uptown Business Women's Club and sang in the choir at Plymouth Congregational Church. She finally retired at age seventy-five when she was stricken with shingles, a painful and, in her case, persistent skin disorder. Around the same time she decided to stop driving. But she established a long list of friends and family on whom she called for rides to activities of all sorts. She wasn't about to stay home just because she couldn't drive.

Always a Republican, she became an outspoken defender of the insurance industry and private enterprise in general. Portraits of Republican leaders, including much-maligned Presidents Herbert Hoover and Richard Nixon, found places of honor in her apartment at the Belmont, at Franklin and Hennepin Avenues.

There was never another man in her life as far as I knew. As she grew older and my brothers all moved to California, she was stuck with me. I looked out for her while trying not to cramp her style. She was sharp, opinionated, and involved in the city she loved until she died in February 1983, at age eighty-eight.

I think kids today are raised with more praise and affection than I was given or than my generation in general received. Ideas about parenting were different then. But I was raised to be responsible, adaptable, hardworking, and successful. That's what Mother was. To the extent that I became those things, I owe it to her.

CHAPTER 2

Student Days

MOST OF MY CHILDHOOD was spent in what is today called the Page neighborhood. It takes its name from Page Elementary School, which in turn was named for Walter Hines Page, a journalist and diplomat who never set foot in Minnesota. He had been the U.S. ambassador to Great Britain during the run-up to World War I and played a major role in getting my dad's generation into that battle.

I didn't know all that when I attended Page Elementary. I just knew that at Page School learning happened in portable buildings that could be moved—and actually were. The school opened in 1925 in portable structures perched on lowlands near Minnehaha Creek. In the summer of 1930, I watched as workmen jacked up those buildings to accommodate dirt that was being moved from the construction site for the new Ramsey Junior High School, a few blocks to the west. Actually, I did more than watch—I sold lemonade to the crew. Those cheap, "temporary" portable classrooms lasted for thirty-three years and were finally replaced with an actual building in 1958. The school itself was used until 1982. In 1984 it was torn down and replaced by town houses.

In 1930, Minneapolis had about 75,000 more residents than it does today, and a lot more of them were children. Schools were crowded. One of the school district's coping mechanisms was to start some kindergarteners in the fall semester and some in late January, leading to a sequence of half-grades labeled A and B. That approach made it easier for good students to skip a semester or two in the sequence and move through more rapidly.

I skipped four half-grades—two full years—as a grade school student. I suppose that was a compliment to my academic ability. But Mom didn't want me to get a big head about that—she told me I was advancing because my teachers could only stand one semester of my talkative nature. I could never tell whether Mom was teasing or sincere, but one piece of evidence was against me. My third-grade teacher, Miss Diamond, once put adhesive tape over my mouth to get me to stop talking.

Semester skipping put me in the first 7B class to enroll in brand-new Ramsey Junior High School in January 1932. It stood next to six-year-old Washburn High School, considered the best in the city—at least by everyone in my neighborhood. I knew I was headed there after junior high. I was only ten years old at the start of junior high, two years younger than many of my peers. If that held me back socially, I wasn't aware of it. That experience plus being the eldest child at home gave me a level of comfort with people older than myself that I think served me well.

The names and history of those two schools gave us students a connection to Minnesota's founding. Ramsey was named for Alexander Ramsey, Minnesota's first territorial governor, second state governor, and most prominent politician in the nineteenth century. Washburn was officially named for William D. Washburn, the youngest brother of a large family from Maine that spawned a number of successful pioneers in the Midwest. The Washburn family nickname for him was "Young Rapid." William D. settled in Minneapolis, went into the railroad and flour milling businesses, built an eighty-room mansion—the largest house in the city, before or since—served in the U.S. Senate, and lost his fortune shortly before he died. But Washburn High School's principal, Archibald Ebenezer MacQuarrie, insisted that the school was named for a more famous older brother, Cadwallader Washburn. Though Cadwallader was governor of Wisconsin and never lived in Minnesota, he was the founder of the Minneapolis milling company today known as General Mills. Ramsey Junior High School (today's Ramsey International Fine Arts Center) was built on the site of one of Cadwallader's posthumous bequests to Minneapolis—an orphanage. Washburn sought to provide for the offspring of workers killed in milling accidents like the massive explosion at his company's "A" Mill in 1878. This bequest survives today as the Washburn Center for Children, with three Twin Cities locations. Principal MacQuarrie was so insistent that his school's name referred to Cadwallader, not Young Rapid, that he kept a picture of Cadwallader on his office wall.

A. E. MacQuarrie was Washburn High School's founding principal and held that post for nineteen years. I thought he owned the place, and he might have thought so too. He lived a block away, between Fiftieth and Fifty-First Streets on Nicollet Avenue, in a big, imposing brick house that bespoke success. MacQuarrie was the school's dominant personality. He had no children of his own; lack of parental experience may have contributed to his stern, no-nonsense attitude toward students.

I got a taste of MacQuarrie's approach to discipline on the day in eleventh-grade geometry when our teacher, Miss Olson, left the room for a moment and some guy threw an eraser at me. I wasn't going to be anybody's target. I picked up the eraser and heaved it back at his head—just as Miss Olson returned to the room. She reported my misdeed to Mr. MacQuarrie. As a result, admission to the National Honor Society was denied to me that spring. That was harsh punishment, and today it would likely bring parents to the principal's office to protest. In 1937, with the Depression in full force, it didn't register a peep with my parents. Dad had bigger troubles that year.

I ran afoul of Principal MacQuarrie again on one of my last days as a senior, in an episode that's seared into my memory. I was a member of Washburn's golf team. I settled for that sport after trying out unsuccessfully for basketball. I had developed an interest in the game while accompanying my parents and brother Bob on summer Sunday afternoons to the University of Minnesota's golf course. The folks would play a round, and Bob and I would caddy for them. Those were pleasant outings. What happened in the state high school golf tournament in 1938 was not.

The tournament was organized as match play. Each school fielded a seven-man team, and each man was paired against a man from the rival school. The winner of each match scored one point for his team. The best four of seven match winners decided the outcome. We had a good team that year and wound up tied for the championship with our archrival, Minneapolis West High School in Uptown. We played a match with West at Meadowbrook Golf

Course to decide the city championship. My West High opponent arrived late for the final eighteen-hole round, so the rest of the pairs were ahead of us. As my opponent and I prepared to tee off on the sixteenth hole, all even in our match, other players from the first six matches came over the hill to tell us that the other six pairs were tied, three to three. The championship depended on the outcome of my contest.

Both my opponent and I kept our cool through holes 16 and 17 and stayed even. But on the eighteenth, both of us lost control. Balls were flying all over the place. A crowd, including my coach and math teacher, Lloyd Alwin, gathered to cheer me on. The pressure grew. We arrived at the green tied. Putting would tell the story. I missed a three-footer to lose the hole, the match, and the city championship. "Damn it!" I said, evidently loud enough for my coach and some in the crowd to hear. Mr. Alwin reported my bad language to Mr. MacQuarrie. Even though I was about to graduate, MacQuarrie suspended me from school for three days for unsportsmanlike conduct. That's how exacting he was.

For solace, I turned to the neighborhood buddies who had been my closest friends throughout elementary and high school. Bob Litman lived across the street from us on Clinton Avenue. His dad was a doctor at the Veteran's Administration Hospital. The family was Jewish, and my respect and affection for him and his family inoculated me against the anti-Semitism that was pervasive in Minneapolis in those years. He went on to be a psychiatrist who treated Hollywood-movie celebrity patients. Even as a kid, he was a good listener and asked good questions.

"What's your middle name?" he once asked when we were pretty small. I didn't know yet that my birth certificate actually said Thomas Jackson Swain. I told him what I'd always been told: my middle name is Holliday. But I thought it was spelled *Holiday*, and so did Bob.

"So you were named Holiday because you were born on the Fourth of July?" he asked.

"Yes," I said confidently. I had bragged as much to others, proud of my personal connection to the nation's Independence Day. But I realized when Bob asked that I wasn't really sure about the origin of my name. I decided to ask my mother.

14

"No, silly. It's not Holiday with one *l*. It's Holliday, my maiden name!" Until then, I was unaware of Mother's family name. I was so embarrassed at the faux pas that I told her that when I was legally able, I intended to change my middle name to Richard. Fortunately, I'd matured a bit by age twenty-one and kept Holliday.

Diagonally across the street was Bob Linderberg, a wonderful fellow who died much too young during the polio epidemic of 1950. A few houses away was Roy Eveland, whose father was a dentist. The four of us had a lot of adventures, not all of them entirely wholesome. By the time we were about thirteen years old, being downtown without parental supervision was routine, as was using the streetcar whenever we pleased. One day Bob Litman and I dared each other to engage in some petty larceny at the downtown Woolworth's five-and-dime on the corner of Seventh Street and Nicollet Avenue. We each smuggled a few clips and rubber bands and dashed out the door, only to be stopped by a policeman. Someone had suspected mischief and tipped off the corner cop. The tip was vague enough that the officer evidently did not know exactly what he was looking for. He decided to frisk two boys and chose Eveland and Linderberg—the ones who had nothing to hide. Bob Litman and I watched in fear as our friends were searched, expecting that we would be next and we would be in big trouble. But inexplicably, the officer stopped after frisking two, and let all of us go. Bob and I were lucky that day. And our panic taught us a lasting lesson even though we weren't caught.

A few years later I was falsely accused of shoplifting at the same downtown corner, Seventh and Nicollet. This time, it was in the men's department at Donaldson's, which was operated by a franchisee named John Chaix. Linderberg figures in this episode. His dad was a representative for a line of upscale men's clothing headquartered in Philadelphia. It happened that most of the samples he was allotted were my size. Knowing that, Bob's dad hired me on several occasions as a model, and he occasionally gave me a garment. That was the case for a topcoat that I wore into Donaldson's one day when I was a freshman in college. Even though people dressed more formally then than they do today, this coat must have seemed too nice to be worn by a seventeen-year-old college kid. When I left the store at the Sixth and Nicollet corner, Chaix stopped me.

He accused me of stealing the coat and demanded to see the label sewn on the inside to prove it. When I refused out of stubbornness, he summoned a policeman standing just outside. The cop asked me to open my coat, and I refused again—so he unbuttoned it for me. The label proved that the coat was mine, not the store's. By this time, a crowd had gathered, and the crowd was clearly siding with me. Chaix beat it back into the men's clothing department without saying a word to me. The policeman did the apologizing and allowed that Chaix had made similar false accusations before. When I heard that, I decided I would not let the matter drop. Somehow I found the nerve to go back into the store, find Chaix, and demand an apology. He mumbled one. Later, an attorney who was a friend of the family said I should have come to him right away to press for financial recompense.

I came to understand Chaix's position a little better a few years later. During my junior and senior years at the university, my athletic department ticket job blossomed into a full-time responsibility for the fall semesters. I manned a small ticket sales booth downtown—right outside Chaix's department. I was alone there and not as careful as I should have been. I once left the booth to go to the bathroom and returned to find my tickets gone. I was reminded that not everyone comes downtown with good intentions.

There was never a question about whether or where this son of a Dinkytown businessman would go to college. After I graduated from Washburn High, the University of Minnesota was my natural next step in the fall of 1938. I just hopped onto the Nicollet Avenue streetcar and enrolled.

The importance of streetcars to Minneapolis life in the first half of the twentieth century may be hard to appreciate for those who became acquainted with the city after the streetcars vanished in 1954. The streetcar was my exclusive form of transportation. I didn't own a car until after World War II. The streetcar gave me independence and a connection to the whole city at a young age. Walking to streetcar stops gave me the habit of daily walks that has served me to this day. Very seldom did I ask my parents for a ride when I wanted to go somewhere. Dad owned a car when I was a teenager, a Viking. It was for his use, which meant that Mother was without a car most of the time. She didn't complain because anywhere she wanted to go, the streetcar could take her. We bought our groceries at Pelling Grocery at Fifty-Third Street and Nicollet, and they were delivered to our house. The local bakery and dairy delivered too. Even liquor stores delivered after Prohibition ended in 1933—not that my parents took advantage of that service. We kids learned the streetcar routes and schedule by heart at a young age. I took the streetcar alone to downtown Westminster Presbyterian Church for Boy Scout meetings when I was about twelve years old. I was familiar with the University of Minnesota campus not only because Dad's business was nearby but because I'd been there many times by streetcar. I enrolled in the university's Institute of Technology (IT) with a vague notion of becoming an engineer. Why engineering? I'll never know.

The student body I joined numbered 14,000, undergraduates plus graduate students. I didn't know many other students, but my job at the athletic ticket office gave me some connections and kept me busy.

The church basketball league that I joined that year did too. Sometime that winter, I was playing at a church in the Uptown area when I came down hard on my knee. I wound up at Eitel Hospital, a small hospital near Loring Park, for a full week, as the doctors tried to stop blood from pooling under my kneecap. I learned much later that my kneecap had been broken. The interruption in my studies meant that I had to drop a class or two. The academic pace was swift in the math and science classes I was taking; there could be no catching up after missing ten days of classes. As I was rearranging my class load, someone suggested that I take an aptitude test. It's among the best advice I have ever received. The person who discussed my test results with me said, "Tom, you'd be a passable engineer at best. You're better suited for business or work in the public sector." Those words rang true to me. It was as if a light had been switched on, showing me my path forward.

That spring, I transferred from IT to the prebusiness track at the university division then called SLA (Science, Literature, and the Arts). Today it's the College of Liberal Arts. It wasn't an entirely easy transition. My English professor, an exacting fellow nearing retirement, told me my syntax was lacking in the papers I wrote. I couldn't tell him that I did not know what syntax was! My first two quarters of freshman English had been in IT where I did papers on the physical dimensions of an auto key case and the part that free throws played in Minneapolis High School basketball games. I decided to withdraw from his class, take an incomplete, and retake it later with a different professor. The next year I enrolled in the class again, and I was assigned the same professor! I didn't have the nerve to take it with him and registered for something else instead. I finally took my last freshman English class as a senior, after the professor who did not like my syntax had retired.

For a little fun, I played duplicate bridge at the old Men's Union, which would be replaced by Coffman Union in 1940. The university had a bridge team that competed in intercollegiate tournaments, and I thought it would be fun to join. Before long, I was elected the team's captain—not because I was particularly good at bridge, but because the other fellows were bashful, nerdy types who didn't want to be a spokesman for the University of Minnesota. The year I was captain, we were invited to compete in a national tournament. We were surprised to come in fourth or fifth place, despite competing against elite schools in the East.

Coffman Union was being built that year. My first contribution of any kind was to the Coffman Union building fund. I gave $20, which was almost the cost of tuition for a quarter then. It felt good.

By my junior year, my responsibilities at the athletic ticket office had grown, and my academic calendar changed accordingly. I attended classes winter and spring quarters and the first summer session, skipping fall quarter. That way I could give full-time attention to ticket sales for University of Minnesota football games—the hottest ticket for any sporting event in town. From the middle of July until the end of the year it was full-time-plus, initially at thirty-five cents per hour. Besides football, I attended to basketball and hockey business. In my senior year I advanced to fifty cents per hour. I was one of only four student employees to attain that lofty level of compensation that year.

Those were the glory years for Bernie Bierman's Gophers. Coach Bierman had become a local hero with his first three national championships, back to back in 1934, 1935, and 1936. His teams won the national title again while I was on the ticket staff, in 1940 and 1941. It was an exciting time to be in and around the Brickhouse, as old Memorial Stadium was called. It was a term of respect and affection. I never understood the criticism of Memorial Stadium that led to the decision in 1982 to move Gopher football into the Hubert H. Humphrey Metrodome. Memorial was built in 1924 and named to honor the students who had served in World War I, including my dad. It could accommodate nearly 62,000 fans on a Saturday afternoon—and in those winning years, it almost always did.

Ticket sales wound down after Thanksgiving, and my academic year started. Soon after winter term started in 1941, I stopped by Desnick Bros. Drug Store one Sunday afternoon to grab a snack and play a hand or two of gin rummy with one of the owners, Baron Desnick. After the family moved to 4525 Nicollet, the drugstore was only a block away from our new home. Riding the streetcar from that new location each day had given me a new circle of somewhat older, working-adult friends who gathered at Desnick's. I had playing cards in my hand that afternoon, December 7, 1941, when a radio announced that Pearl Harbor was under attack. I was twenty years old. The draft had just ended and had spared me. Military service was the furthest thing from my mind until that moment. When I heard the news, I knew something big had happened that would affect me.

The U.S. entry into World War II was one of two things that happened during my senior year that shaped my life after graduation. The second was much more under my control. I joined a fraternity, Theta Chi. Its members had been rushing me for some time, and I'd been interested in them because of their house's connection to my dad. During his one year at the University of Minnesota, he had been part of the Thulanian Club, a social group of Norwegian origin whose members included two future Minnesota governors, J. A. O. Preus and Theodore Christianson. That club morphed into the Alpha Pi chapter of Theta Chi, a national fraternity, in 1924. It was large and financially solid enough to build a big house near campus at 315 Sixteenth Avenue SE. Living at that house was expensive. I hesitated to join because of the cost. But one could join without moving into the house, and that's what I finally did.

Fraternities are supposed to provide a family of sorts for lonely college students. I wasn't exactly lonely. But I suppose that after my dad's disappearance two years before, I was missing something. Theta Chi gave me thirty-one "brothers." One of them, Harry Reasoner, went on to national prominence as a television news broadcaster. Three of them would be killed in combat in World War II. One of those three was my closest friend, Don Garniss.

I knew Don a bit at Washburn High School. Though we were about the same age, he was two years behind me as a result of my semester skipping in elementary school. Don was an all-round good guy and a letterman in swimming. He was also principled, willing to speak up in defense when someone was being criticized. I liked that about him, and we clicked. His roommate at the Theta Chi house was the fraternity's president, Gus Cooper. Gus looked out for Don like a big brother. Don returned the favor by introducing Gus to his sister, whom Gus eventually married. Don also introduced me to his girlfriend, Arlene McWilliams. As I said, he was a good guy.

Don and I decided to enlist in the U.S. Navy together in the summer of 1942. We envisioned serving on the daring new PT boats that the Navy was using to attack and sink larger vessels and that became famous a few decades later when a PT boat veteran, John F. Kennedy, was elected president. But the Navy wouldn't have me, and the reason was a surprise. Navy screeners discovered that I am color-blind, which made me unacceptable at that time. Don wound up in the Army Air Corps; I enlisted in the Army Reserve Corps and was subject to being called up on short notice. I suppose I was a bit disappointed; many of my friends were older and already in uniform. But enlisting in the reserves enabled me to finish my accounting degree requirements and graduate from the university in December 1942. That time also allowed me to deepen my connection to Theta Chi. I was the chapter's treasurer, which is why I still remember that on my watch, Harry Reasoner never paid the chapter the $69.50 he owed us when he graduated. My responsibilities included acting as the chapter house's business manager, renting rooms to graduate students attending summer school.

After graduation, I looked for a job suitable for a guy with a freshly minted accounting degree who could be called into military service at any moment. I found one that was considered a plum in Rockford, Illinois, at that city's branch of the Philadelphia accounting firm Lybrand, Ross Bros. and Montgomery. The firm was founded in 1898 and by 1942 was among the nation's leaders in accounting. It's one of the predecessor firms of today's PricewaterhouseCoopers, or PwC. Rockford was and is a manufacturing town. In the fall of 1942 its factories were operating at full capacity to produce war matériel under government contracts. I was assigned to start auditing their books right away.

It wasn't all green-eyeshade office work. I was assigned to check the books of a coal company in southern Illinois and found myself walking around and measuring cylindrical piles of coal. I used an old Boy Scout trick to calculate for myself the volume of coal in those piles and impressed their owners with how near I came to their own figures. In Freeport, Illinois, I visited a company that was making torpedoes. Its workers were spray painting them without wearing masks—a hazard to their lungs. When I pointed that out, the company managers thanked me. The sincerity of that response made it memorable. Some employers really do care about the welfare of their workers.

I had been told to expect a call from the Army at any time, so I opted for temporary living arrangements in Rockford and getting around by train and bus. I still had no car. The call finally came in February 1943. I was Private Thomas H. Swain, serial number 17114071, in the Army Air Corps.

CHAPTER 3

Staff Sergeant Swain

"**G**IMME ME HAT. Me's goin' out." That was how the guy in the sack next to mine greeted me as I prepared for my first night of basic training in a second-floor barracks at Sheppard Air Field in February 1943. Sheppard was in Wichita Falls, Texas, on the south bank of the Red River that forms the border between Texas and Oklahoma. As I handed my barracks mate the hat he sought, one fact hit home: I was no longer at the University of Minnesota. I had entered a very different environment.

My unfamiliarity with the ways of the U.S. Army Air Corps seemed almost matched by its uncertainty about how to make use of me. I was only twenty-one, not much older than many of the other raw recruits in basic training. But I was one of very few to arrive with a college degree. In the years before the GI Bill, only 5 percent of American high school graduates went to college. The drill sergeant was a guy named Olson, to whom I took a liking. He'd bark at me by day, then play cards with me at night. He cheated, and I enjoyed the challenge of figuring out how he did it. I noticed that as our games continued, his daytime vocabulary became more like mine. One day he hollered, "Get those beds as close to the wall as the confirmation will permit!" He evidently was studying me too.

The Army wasn't racially integrated in those years—and neither was the Minneapolis of my youth. African Americans had been living in the city since its founding, but by the 1920s, real estate redlining had effectively confined them to about five of the city's thirteen wards, none of them frequented by me. But my awareness of the nation's racial divide was quickening, and an episode in downtown Wichita Falls toward the end of basic training advanced my understanding of the damage that divide did to African American psyches. A few of us on a pass went to town for a few hours one night and were walking along a sidewalk. A black man appeared from between two buildings just ahead of us. When he saw us, he immediately jumped back into the space from which he had come. Evidently, he had been conditioned to give white men the right of way and avoid any possible accusation that he was impeding our movement. It was a gesture of such subservience that it made me uncomfortable. My sense of justice was stirred.

I also trace my aversion to waiting in lines, any lines, to basic training at Sheppard. We got paid $50 a month. Once a month, after evening chow, an entire squadron was directed to line up alphabetically to sign the payroll. A week later, once again, we formed an alphabetical line to collect our money. A squadron was about 5,000 guys. A name beginning with *Sw* put me far back in line. Of the $50, I had arranged to send a $22 allotment to my mother. They made us buy a U.S. savings bond—that was $18.75. It was $6.60 for life insurance. I wasn't going to do my own laundry; that was another $1.50. The upshot was that I had to stand in line after chow for four or five hours to sign up to get $1.15. A week later I had to stand in line another four or five hours to receive it. To this day, I hate standing in lines.

I was stalled at Sheppard longer than most as the Air Corps pondered where to send me. My wait continued at my next stop, a troop replacement depot in Salt Lake City. Finally I got the word: they wanted me in the Finance Corps because I had been an accounting major at the University of Minnesota. That was the last thing I wanted! I wanted something more active, maybe involving a little adventure. Dragging my feet, I boarded a train to Pyote Army Air Field, in dusty, hot, middle-of-nowhere West Texas. The town was so small that when the Texas and Pacific passenger trains stopped there, both ends of the train were out of town. Rattlesnakes outnumbered humans in Pyote before Uncle Sam decided it should be the site of the nation's largest bomber flight training installation. We GIs called the place Rattlesnake Army Air Base and took to hanging each day's catch of dead rattlesnakes over the front gate as a warning to uninitiated newcomers: Beware! Keep your leggings on!

Most of the arrivals in 1943 were pilots, bombardiers, navigators, radio operators, and gunners who were to be assembled into crews for B-17 Flying Fortresses. I was a member of the Finance Corps, assigned to sit at the front counter of the Finance Building and advise new officers, many of them from humble backgrounds, about how to open a bank account and manage their $152 per month salaries. I didn't much care for that work, and maybe because I was unhappy, I got crosswise with my unit head, Capt. Eugene Taber. That made me unhappier still.

Then rescue came. Warrant Officer Tom Kleppe was from Bismarck, North Dakota, and had worked for Gold Seal Wax before the war. He took notice of me and concluded that I might solve a problem with the operation of the Pyote's Officers' Club mess and BOQ, the bachelor officers' quarters. He got me transferred as the accountant and office manager for those facilities. The job essentially involved running a combination club, casino, cafeteria, and dormitory for officers.

It wasn't the adventure I was seeking, but at least I could use what I'd learned in college to solve a genuine business problem. I applied common sense and got things straightened out in a hurry. One room at the club was entirely filled with slot machines. Many of the new officers had nothing else to do but pump nickels, dimes, and quarters into those machines. These things were so popular that some officers would hire someone to pull the handles for them so they could keep playing when their arms grew weary. The machines got such a workout that one man's entire job was repairing broken slot machines. The machines' payout was governed by the number of lemons in the first reel. When I arrived, the machines had only one lemon in the first reel. Payouts were high. I replaced them with machines with either three or five lemons on the first reel. The payout was greatly reduced, and the club's revenues improved dramatically. During the sixteen months I was there, we used that revenue to build a new officers' club, bowling alley, and enlisted men's club, with some to spare. Our business model drew recognition all over the Second Air Force in the western United States.

My office was in a corner of the officers' mess hall, which was a cafeteria open twenty-four hours a day because training flights were occurring at all hours, and it was staffed by African Americans—the acceptable term then was "coloreds." Early in my assignment, I was in my office quite late one night when a couple of majors from the training group entered. Both were intoxicated, one obviously more than the other. The more impaired one went after one of the men behind the counter with terrible, extreme racial slurs. It got me out of my office.

I noticed that there weren't many others in the mess hall just then. A few waiters had witnessed the verbal assault. They'd stopped working and were beginning to react. Concerned for their safety, I hollered at them, "Get back to your work."

Then I went to the two majors and said, "We can't serve you."

"The hell you can't," they countered.

I tried to convince the companion of the verbally abusive major that he should take his friend elsewhere. He refused. Then somebody called the MPs, the military police. I was a private; they were majors. They made their case to the MPs, and I wound up spending the night in the guardhouse.

But that injustice produced a positive result. By morning, other officers who had been eating there and witnessed the episode had spoken up on my behalf. I was out of trouble. And I became a respected figure among the African American staff at the club and mess hall, which paid dividends for me for the rest of my stay at Pyote.

While I was there, I was made an acting master sergeant because I was working in an officers' unit. That rank brought a raise in pay. I gained $72 per month, half of a master sergeant's $144 pay, in addition to my private's pay. While still in Pyote, I was officially promoted to corporal.

In June 1944, my mother contacted me with terrible news. My best college friend Don Garniss was missing in action. He was a B-24 bomber pilot who, with his squadron, had performed a mission in Nazi-occupied northern France in May 1944. His plane sustained some damage. On their way back to their base in Italy, he signaled the squadron leader that his plane could not stay with the group. It went down in the Mediterranean, just off the coast of France. Eyewitnesses reported seeing a number of parachutes, but no survivors were found. Don was declared missing in action, implying some official hope that he might have survived. But in World War II, an MIA designation often meant that there had been a death, but no body could be found to confirm it. After a soldier had been missing in action for a year, he or she would be declared dead.

Don's disappearance was made all the more painful by the knowledge that he was a young husband who had just become a father. Don married Arlene McWilliams in Bainbridge, Georgia, in May 1943. On April 3, 1944, their daughter Jo Anne was born. I sat down at a typewriter on June 16 and wrote to the young woman Don and his friends called Mac to try to express my condolences. "You used to ride him about being in love with me and not paying any attention to you," I wrote. "You were wrong in the way you stated that. But if you can use the word 'love' to describe friendship and companionship in the highest degree that a guy holds for a fellow man, you can use it in depicting the way I feel about Don. That probably sounds wishy-washy, but by God, I mean it. There isn't a finer fellow on the face of the earth." I took care to use present tense to describe Don. I told Arlene that I did not believe he was gone. But the bloody madness of World War II had a way of stripping its participants of their optimism.

I genuinely cared about Arlene and her baby daughter. "Please write to me and let me know what you're thinking," I wrote. "I may not be able to be of any help, but I'll certainly do my damnedest trying. There isn't anything in the world I wouldn't do for you. We've had a hell of a lot of spats, but I think you know me as well as any other person does. Inherently, my heart's in the right spot. . . . I'm with you all of the way." Those words were truer than I knew.

I shared with Arlene my frustration at spending the war that would define my generation as the manager of a stateside officers' club and mess. I made efforts to transfer to other units that would offer an opportunity for more meaningful service, including volunteering for the Army Air Force emergency rescue boat crews and asking for a transfer to the infantry. But I was told that I had been designated "key personnel" by someone in Pyote who liked the way I ran the officers' club and wanted to keep me there. It did keep me busy. I had very few nights off.

One of them gave me a bit of adventure, although not the kind I was craving. I was in nearby Monahans, Texas, which is bigger than Pyote but still a small town. Along with a couple of other fellows, I ran into my officers' club superior, Frank Penny, a good guy. He invited me to join his group and bought me a beer or two. We had a pleasant chat—so pleasant that time got away from me. As an enlisted man, I faced an 11:00 P.M. curfew. Penny was an officer who had no curfew. The MPs swooped in and nailed me. I was taken to the military detention facility and settled in for the night. But someone in the place set his mattress on fire. "We're going to get you the hell out of here," the MPs running the jail said as they hastily released me and ordered me to go back to the base. The next day I had to appear before our unit's commander, Major Swingle. His judgment: I'd already paid a sufficient price for my transgression. "Go about your business," he said. I liked Swingle and looked up to him, thinking of him as an older and wiser man. He was probably about thirty-five.

Finally, one of my bids to volunteer for the infantry got someone's attention. After sixteen months in Pyote, I was sent to Great Bend, Kansas, to join the 333rd Bomb Group. First, I was allowed a brief furlough. It was a chance to reconnect with family and friends—and to stock up on provisions that would be hard to find in "dry" Kansas. I bought a case of whiskey and wrapped it in underwear and towels in my big, now-heavy barracks bag. When I left Minneapolis, I went to Toledo, Ohio, to visit a woman I'd met in Pyote. That was an ill-fated relationship that I remember now for the pain involved in lugging my heavy barracks bag from Minneapolis to Chicago to Toledo, then back to Chicago. There I had to transfer to a train to Great Bend, which was so crowded that I had to stand the whole way. That was hard. But boy, was I a hero when I got to the barracks and opened that bag!

My plan in Great Bend was to train to be a B-29 gunner. But I'd hardly begun when I was detached again. Major Magimelli had been in Pyote. He was head of a unit in the 316th Bomb Wing (VH) in Colorado Springs, preparing to go overseas and searching for someone to run an officers' club. He found me in Great Bend. The next thing I knew, I was on my way to Colorado Springs for more officers' club duty. At least Colorado Springs was a nicer place than Pyote, and I wasn't there long. My unit's next assignment was in the South Pacific, and I was ordered to set up an officers' club wherever we went. I also went with a higher rank, as a sergeant.

Part of the preparation for the overseas assignment involved receiving an inoculation for bubonic plague. The Army was using a new serum, and it was tested on us. About half of us wound up in the hospital. I didn't, but I was plenty sick, as were my barracks mates. Some officer came into the barracks and ordered us to get up and work. We moaned, "Do whatever you want to us. We can't get up." That shot slowed our preparations considerably.

My travel itinerary in early 1945 sent me from Colorado Springs to Seattle, then to the South Pacific aboard the USS *Carteret*, a slow two-stacker. It took us fifty-four days to get to our eventual destination, Okinawa. We had a weeklong layover in Pearl Harbor. The officers were allowed to come and go as they pleased, but enlisted men were ordered not to leave the ship. It was unbearably hot in the below-deck sleeping quarters. Some of us took to sleeping on the deck. Some Navy guy from Wisconsin saved me by inviting me to use a berth where the Navy guys slept that was much more comfortable. We played endless games of Hearts to pass the time.

One of our stops was at tiny Mogmog in the Ulithi Islands. The scene there was impressive. Hundreds of U.S. naval vessels of all kinds were anchored there in a huge basin. While there, we enlisted men had a drawing to see who would be permitted the first day off the ship. I drew it. Immediately I was inundated with offers to trade that day off for amazingly rich loot. Those fellows were desperate to get off that ship—but so was I. No trade. But my day off was no luxury tour. I was hauled to shore in a crowded pontoon-style boat, herded through a receiving area that reminded me of the South St. Paul stockyards, and guided to a makeshift ball field where warm beer was available and about 150 guys were trying to play one game of softball. It was dismal.

After another delay in Tinian, an island that the Allies wrested from Japan in a bloody fight in mid-1944, we finally arrived at our destination, Kadena Airfield on Okinawa. It was mid-April, and a battle was still in progress on the south end of the long, narrow island. Allied troops had invaded at about the midpoint of the Japanese-held island on Easter Sunday, April 1, 1945. They took control of Kadena on the first day and met little resistance as they moved northward, but they encountered stubborn opposition from small but heavily entrenched Japanese forces as they moved south. Allied military masterminds insisted that the Japanese be completely routed. We could have simply contained them, with much less loss of U.S. life. Instead, America lost 12,500 young lives on Okinawa before the fighting ended in June. It was America's bloodiest battle against Japan, causing double the losses sustained in the more infamous island battle on Iwo Jima.

I was out of harm's way—at least of the man-made sort. I was part of a headquarters unit, serving four operational squadrons from a secured airfield in the middle of the island. We maintained constant guard around our complexes at night, and I took my turn as sergeant of the guard on night duty. But I never faced a threatening situation.

We settled in at Kadena for what we expected to be a long stay. The United States was preparing for an invasion of Japan. Okinawa was only 340 miles south of the enemy's homeland, closer than any other Allied base in the South Pacific. We would have been the invasion's launching pad. That made news of the U.S. use of atomic bombs in Hiroshima and Nagasaki personal to us. Japan surrendered on August 15.

The run-up to the signing of the peace treaty on the battleship *Missouri* was a jubilant time. Some Okinawa Marines started firing weapons—more than just rifles—and weren't careful about their aim. A few rounds went in the direction of some U.S. Navy battleships in the harbor. The Navy did not care who was shooting. They were under attack and fired back. That was the only time during the entire war that I went into a foxhole.

The war was over, but typhoon season had begun. Nature was about to show us that an occupying military force can encounter more than one kind of danger. As Typhoon Louise approached, the commander of the 316th, Colonel DuBose, ordered that Kadena Airfield squad tents be secured in a way that would withstand any storm, no matter how severe. As the ranking noncommissioned officer in my ten-man tent, I took that order to heart and got my tent mates busy putting up additional beams and poles to reinforce our humble shelter.

As I participated in those preparations, I also was busy with an assignment of my own instigation. I had the idea that our mimeographed daily base newsletter, the *Kadena Strip*, should cover the World Series then being played between the Chicago Cubs and the Detroit Tigers. I went to the Special Services officer, Lt. R. F. Merritt, with a proposal: We've got a shortwave radio, and our clocks lag those in Detroit and Chicago by twelve hours. We could pick up the games at night via shortwave installation in our unit and have the results in our newsletter on breakfast tables the next morning for everybody in the Eighth Air Force. Merritt was skeptical, but when I volunteered for duty as the sleepless sportswriter, he agreed.

The game reports were a big hit. The fun I had keeping a running tally of the action, inning by inning, and compiling a box score made up (mostly) for the sleep I missed. Merritt helped, keeping me awake and getting the mimeograph stencil prepared when I had the copy ready. It was a lively series that went to seven games. But the morning after the Cubs tied the series in game six, my story was pushed off the newsletter's front page by the headline "Typhoon Here Head-on." Its peak winds were due that afternoon.

Typhoon Louise was moderate by Okinawa standards, but it produced winds gusting up to 85 miles per hour that no tent could withstand, no matter what a colonel said. My tent had the dubious distinction of being the last to fall. We had a big mess on our hands. At the height of the storm, I somehow commandeered an ambulance—the only enclosed vehicle I could find—and steered sideways, crab-style, down a muddy road to rescue as much of our stuff as I could. With no tents left on the island and replacement tents a few days away in the Philippines, I was able to stash some things in a crowded Quonset hut, but I was obliged to sleep outside in the mud.

There was no baseball game that night because it was a travel day for the Tigers and Cubs. If there had been a game, it would have been tough to cover. The base was so disrupted that my stint as a baseball writer seemed to be over. But Merritt relished the positive recognition my World Series coverage brought him, and he wasn't going to let a little typhoon stop us. I was asleep in the mud for the second night when Merritt found me. He'd found operational radios, he said, and we were going to cover Game Seven. We did—and Merritt got promoted as a result.

Sportswriting wasn't the only unusual duty that befell me on Okinawa in the months after hostilities ceased. I was also tapped to be Cupid's helper. Ours was a headquarters group, heavy with senior officers. It also included an all-female civilian Red Cross unit. In a nasty incident elsewhere on the island, an American military woman was assaulted. A new regulation was issued: Female personnel were not to travel at night on the island without a minimum of two armed men in tow. Only main highways were to be used by vehicles transporting a woman. Parking—a term with multiple meanings where dating was concerned—was strictly prohibited.

Those rules presented a new challenge to the amorous. But the war was over, and romance could no longer be contained, either stateside or in the South Pacific. Some of the officers had liaisons with the Red Cross women. On a number of occasions, I was recruited in the evening to accompany an officer and his lady friend so that they would not run afoul of the two-guards rule. We'd find a secluded place to stop, and I'd make myself scarce for a time to provide the couple some privacy. It was not exactly noble duty, but I liked knowing that officers trusted me to be discreet about a matter of personal delicacy. I did not come home with combat experience, but I gained friends.

The Army used a system of points called the Advanced Service Rating Score to determine when to ship soldiers back stateside. My relatively short stay on Okinawa and the facts that I had seen no combat and did not have children waiting for me at home meant I had a long wait. Finally in February 1946 my points were sufficient, and I packed my gear to go home. At the officers' club, I had a large quantity of golf balls made with synthetic rubber. They were prized items because both synthetic and natural rubber supplies had been diverted from civilian to military uses during the war. I decided to take some golf balls home and wound up with two bulging, heavy barracks bags. It wasn't a smart choice. I was obliged to walk half a mile to the ship that would take me home, the USS *Grant*. Navy guys lined the sidewalks, knowing that there would be guys like me trying to carry more than they could handle. These guys weren't aiming to be helpful—they were there to pick over and pilfer jettisoned items. I was straining, but I didn't want those vultures to get my golf balls. Fortunately, one of my tent mates, a burly fellow, saw me struggling and came to my rescue. He carried one of my bags to the ship. I can't remember his name, but I remain grateful to this day. When I got to Seattle, before taking the train to Camp McCoy in Wisconsin for discharge, I mailed one of those barracks bags home to Minneapolis. I wasn't far behind.

CHAPTER 4

Back to Campus

THREE YEARS IS A LONG TIME to be away from home. When the three years were 1943 to 1946, when the whole world changed and I suppose I did too, the home to which I returned was both familiar and foreign. My mother had moved from Forty-Fifth Street and Nicollet Avenue to 4605 Blaisdell Avenue S., mostly to get away from clanging streetcars. She was no longer a displaced homemaker struggling to raise teenaged sons; she was a moderately successful businesswoman and mother of four grown sons, three of whom had served and helped her financially during the war. (My brother Joe, a very slender fellow, was unable to serve in the military because of what was diagnosed as tuberculosis of the spine. When he had some of my pants altered to fit him, the back pockets met! He lived with my mother until after the war, then moved to California.) I moved in with Mom for a time but looked for more independence.

I gravitated to my old stomping ground, the University of Minnesota. It was teeming with returning veterans, and spring quarter would begin on April 1. I had just enough time to enroll in graduate school in pursuit of an MBA degree. With no job prospect in sight, more study seemed like the thing to do. But spring quarter wasn't far along when a tempting job opportunity appeared. Some of those returning vets had been good Golden Gopher football players before the war, when the football program was rather indifferent to its players' academic progress. Two of them, Herb Hein and Herman Frickey, a future coach at Hibbing High School, were dismayed to discover that although they had taken classes for three years before the war, academically they were only second-quarter sophomores. Now older and wiser, they informed Coach Bierman and athletic director Frank McCormick that they were willing to join the football team again provided they could be assured that they and other players would be able to keep pace academically. Playing football should not be an impediment to timely graduation, they argued. They wanted better academic counseling.

McCormick remembered me from my years in the ticket office. He contacted me and offered to make me the university's athletic scholastic adviser, a brand-new position. My assignment was to get players to satisfy the academic eligibility requirements for university athletes. Today they have an army of staffers doing that work. Mine was a solo act. I liked the idea of starting something new in a familiar setting, the athletic fields and offices that had been my haunts as an undergraduate. I threw myself into the role—so much so that my graduate school career lasted only one semester, during which I earned two Bs and two incompletes.

During the 1946–47 school year I worked with some Gopher football stars, including 1946 MVP Billy Bye, a future WCCO broadcaster and coach for Edina High School, and three-sport letterman Bud Grant, the future coach of the Minnesota Vikings. Their standing with the team was never in doubt. I took pride in more complicated cases. Three players in that category were Leo Nomellini, Verne Gagne, and Bob Carley.

Leo was born in Italy and raised in Illinois by a mother who ran a roadside tavern. He didn't play high school football because he had to go home after school and help his mother. But he was a big, strong guy, 250 pounds, and a Chicago general contractor who enjoyed playing talent scout for the Gophers convinced Coach Bierman that Nomellini had great football potential. His academic potential was less apparent. I had to get him into and through some classes.

Nomellini didn't exhibit a lot of academic curiosity. How about psychology? I suggested. "Psy-what? Hell, no!" was his response. How about a little philosophy? "Phi-what? Hell, no!"

"Well, what do you want to take?" I asked.

"How about Spanish?"

"Why Spanish?" I asked. "That's a tough subject."

"I'm from Italy, and that's next door to Spain," he said.

Leo flunked Spanish. But he tried again, applied himself, and became eligible. He joined Theta Delta Chi fraternity, became its president, became an All-American, went into wrestling, married the daughter of a prominent Twin Cities restaurateur, was drafted by the San Francisco 49ers, and wound up playing fourteen seasons and winning All-Pro honors. He was a classic example of someone who likely would never have gone to college or had the successful career he enjoyed had it not been for his presumed athletic potential.

Verne Gagne graduated from Robbinsdale High School in 1943. He was a good football player but was confined to the freshman team in a year when he and every other able-bodied male student expected to be summoned shortly into military service. To put it mildly, he was not a very diligent student in General College. He became ineligible for football and wound up in the Marine Corps. When Gagne returned in 1946, his ineligibility remained in force. Bernie Bierman told me about Gagne and said, "Tom, see what you can do."

General College had co-deans during that period. I paid them a visit. Both of them knew about Gagne and had similar opinions about him. "He's stupid," one said. He'll get readmitted over our collective dead bodies, the other made clear. But I learned that while Gagne was waiting to be discharged from the service, he had enrolled in a couple of correspondence classes offered by San Diego State University. That was the evidence I needed to persuade these deans that Gagne was a new, more mature man and deserved a second chance. After I made several attempts at persuasion, the deans finally relented. "Verne, I've got this wired. Don't screw this up," I said to him as we walked together to the Dean's Office soon thereafter. I didn't mention the opinions the deans held about him.

Verne cleaned up his act, became an NCAA championship wrestler and popular professional wrestler, and eventually founded the American Wrestling Association. I would occasionally see him at Bernie Bierman reunions. After a couple of drinks one night, I let it slip that the General College co-deans had called him stupid.

"Tom, next time you see those fellas, tell them 'twenty grand a week,'" he said, pointing at himself with a big smile.

Bob Carley was a special case and not just because he was a very good multisport athlete. He had been deaf since birth. Adopted into a family in St. Paul, he studied at schools for the deaf in St. Louis and Faribault, where he became an exceptional lip-reader. Even more amazing was that he learned to speak quite well, despite having never heard a word spoken to him. One of the other players told me that one of his great thrills in life was double-dating with Carley and his date when Carley drove. The thrill wasn't a positive one. While Bob was behind the wheel, he periodically turned around to see what the others were saying. He played end on the football team. He had to get practically under the quarterback to be able to read the signals. When he played hockey, the other players would get his attention by pounding their sticks on the ice close to him.

Carley was in the School of Business, where he excelled at mathematical courses but struggled in lecture classes. He'd tend to sit in the back row, where he could not read lips as well but where he could "whisper" to his buddies. Unable to hear his own voice, Carley basically had one volume level, and it wasn't a whisper. As a result, in the spring of 1946, he flunked the Production Management class that was taught by Prof. George Filipetti—who was already showing his age when I took Production Management from him in 1941 or 1942. Coach Bierman asked me, "What can you do?"

I learned that Filipetti was teaching Production Management again in the first summer session in Vincent Hall, one of the stately buildings that fronted on the campus mall. Filipetti remembered Bob and was willing to work with me to give him a second chance. I convinced two other football players, Chuck Delago, a guard, and Bob Sandberg, a quarterback, to take Filipetti's course with Bob and to sit on either side of him in the front row, right in front of Filipetti. I checked in every week.

Things went well until about week five. I got an agitated call from Filipetti. He was so distraught that I could barely understand him, but I caught the word "Carley." I raced over to Vincent Hall from my office in Cooke Hall. What I discovered was that when Filipetti concluded his lecture and the bell rang, Carley did not join the other students exiting the classroom by its only door. Instead, he turned, ran a few steps, and dove out an open window! Filipetti, who usually taught on the second floor, presumed that Carley's stunt had left him badly injured. But this classroom was on the first floor. While Carley got scratched up a bit by the bushes outside the window, he wasn't really hurt. He explained that he had become so tired of being in that classroom on a summer day that he couldn't wait to get out of there. He did it for fun. Boy, I had a time convincing Filipetti that he ought to be allowed to finish the class!

Carley became an All–Big Ten football player and a Gophers hockey star. He would have been a star in the National Hockey League, too, were it not for an injury at practice that cost him vision in his left eye. Eventually he became a coach for his alma mater, St. Paul Academy, where among the players he coached was my son, Tom "Spike" Swain.

Not all of my interventions were as successful. For example, I pushed my friend Stan Wenberg, the head of admissions, to admit a fellow from Chicago named Dick Peot. Peot had come highly recommended as a football player, but his other credentials were shaky. Wenberg relented and attended games that fall hoping to see Peot in action, since I'd blown him up so much. Peot finally came onto the field close to the end of the season, played two plays, got smacked, and never played again.

It wasn't all joy. But after the war, it was good to be connected again to my school. I even lived on campus—actually, right across the street. I became the financial and alumni adviser for my fraternity, Theta Chi, for the 1946–47 school year. That position came with a room in the chapter house and responsibility as an in-house adult counselor to ranks that swelled considerably with the arrival of former GIs to campus. Memories of my fraternity best friend Don Garniss were never far away. Neither was his widow Arlene.

CHAPTER 5

Mac

ARLENE McWILLIAMS GARNISS—"Mac"—and I corresponded regularly after her husband Don went missing in mid-1944. These weren't love letters—not consciously so on my part, anyway. Judging from her casual responses and her mention of other suitors, she wasn't thinking about me romantically either. But we confided in each other with increasing ease, and our friendship deepened. When I returned from the Pacific I was particularly eager to see her and little Jo Anne, who was almost two years old. They were living with Arlene's sister Marilyn and mother, Bertha Merritt McWilliams, at 3708 Pillsbury Avenue S. in Minneapolis.

After that first visit, I wanted more. That meant exercising the knowledge of the Minneapolis streetcar system that I had acquired as a kid because I still didn't own a car. I would get on the Oak-Harriet streetcar, which made a turn at Fifteenth Avenue and Fourth Street SE in Dinkytown. It went downtown, where I could transfer to the Nicollet Avenue line. I would get off at Thirty-Seventh Street and walk two blocks to Pillsbury Avenue to pick up Mac. We'd walk back to Nicollet, get on the streetcar to go downtown, see a movie, then head to the Club Bar for a beer and a sandwich. Beginning at midnight, all the streetcars lined up to make runs that left downtown on the hour all night long. We'd take the midnight run back to Thirty-Seventh and Nicollet, I'd walk her home, kiss her goodnight, and be back at Thirty-Seventh and Nicollet in time (most nights, anyway) to catch the car headed back downtown. It felt like I spent half my life on the streetcar.

That was our pattern for months. At first, I wasn't the only fellow taking her out. But our relationship evolved. I can't say that there was one moment when I ceased thinking of her as my friend and began to think of her as a partner for life. But once that idea dawned, it stuck. I asked her recently what it was that turned me from friend to future husband in her mind. She had a one-word answer: "Persistence."

One key to our relationship has always been Arlene's unabashed way of speaking her mind. We've always had what I call spirited conversations. She is outgoing, warmhearted, and witty, yet her teasing could have a sharp edge. Bright and well informed, she could hold her own in any argument. She holds to high principles and morals. Her political views are more liberal than mine—not greatly so, but enough to keep things interesting. She could always tell when I was bluffing. I found our conversations amusing and intellectually challenging. I think she would have made a fine college debater if she'd had the chance to attend more than a year of college.

But as the youngest daughter in a large family headed by a single mother, Mac wasn't permitted that opportunity. Her income was needed at home. After a year at the University of Minnesota, she went to work at an ammunition plant in Rosemount. An absent father was something Mac and I had in common, though she lost her father much earlier in life than I did. Bert McWilliams was a severe alcoholic, and Bertha banished him—even though that decision left her alone with seven children, six daughters and one son. Arlene never spoke about her father. Once at a six-sister gathering hosted by our daughter Mary, she posed a question about their father to the group. Sister Mildred responded sharply, "We don't talk about him!" That ended the discussion. (Millie Jeffrey was a nationally known union organizer and civil rights activist in Michigan. That's a later story.)

Bertha was better prepared to support her family than my mother was when my dad disappeared. A native of Iowa, Bertha was a pharmacist, the first licensed female pharmacist in the state of Minnesota. Her husband was also a pharmacist, and together they founded McWilliams Drug Store at Forty-Sixth Street and Bryant Avenue in 1923. When the marriage ended, Bertha kept the business alive with some help from her kids. Her corner store still stands and is now occupied by a picture framing shop. Like my mother, Bertha was a gifted woman who worked hard, kept her family together, and earned her way without fuss or drama. She was frugal and never owned a car. I admired her very much. Arlene sometimes said that I married her because of my affection for her mother. That's not quite true—but we did have a great relationship.

As Mac and I became more serious about each other, we included Jo Anne in our time together. Those activities finally got me thinking that I ought to own a car. Transporting a small child is easier in a car. But the car I came up with was no luxury model. It was a thirteen-year-old 1934 Plymouth that I bought for $400. It had a cloth top, which I reinforced with a few layers of six-inch-wide 3M masking tape.

That car caused a series of adventures. One day I picked up Arlene and Jo Anne at Thirty-Seventh Street and Pillsbury Avenue and headed south to Thirty-Eighth Street, where there was a stop sign. I braked. The car didn't. We sailed through the stop sign, fortunately without causing an accident. "What are you doing?" Arlene squealed in alarm. Once on University Avenue, a wheel fell off. I had to dodge traffic on that busy street to retrieve it. During another rush hour in St. Paul, on steep Kellogg Boulevard near the Cathedral of St. Paul, the line from the gas tank to the fuel pump broke. The car stalled in the middle of heavy traffic, and I had a long, nasty wait for help.

The back bumper of this car had a tendency to fall off. I became acquainted with one garage man, Joe Niedoroski on Cedar Street in St. Paul, who was willing to weld that thing back on. It was so near to the gas tank that most other auto body mechanics wouldn't do it. Joe reattached it several times, and each time I rewarded him with a few beers at a bar on Wabasha Avenue.

Arlene and I were married on June 19, 1947, at Incarnation Catholic Church at Thirty-Eighth Street and Pleasant Avenue, a short walk from the McWilliams home. Arlene was Catholic; I was not. That meant that I couldn't walk through the front door of the church for my own wedding. Such discrimination against non-Catholics was not unusual for Catholic parishes in the years before the Vatican II conferences in the 1960s, when the Roman Catholic Church eased some of its restrictive rules. In order to be married there at all, I had to take instruction in Catholicism from Father Frank Fenlon, one of the associate pastors. I enjoyed those sessions and was pleased when Father Fenlon told me at the end that our conversations went on longer than most such sessions because I asked interesting questions. He married us. I would have liked a longer relationship with him, but sadly, he was a victim of the 1950 polio epidemic, was severely handicapped, and died not long after.

Our wedding reception was at Arlene's home. One of my great coups is that I hired a moving van to take the furniture out of the living room. The movers put the furniture in their truck the morning of the wedding and returned it the next morning. The reception involved Arlene and me standing in a receiving line and greeting our guests. Joe Christiansen, the husband of Arlene's closest Central High School friend Verna, kept refilling the nearby punchbowl with products that had been illegal during Prohibition. Arlene was evidently pretty thirsty. When we left the house to party with friends closer to our age at the Curtis Hotel, she had a good head start on the celebrating. One of the fellows there was a former boyfriend. He and Arlene chatted, and the next thing I knew, she had invited him to visit us while we were on our honeymoon at Madden's Resort on Gull Lake, near Brainerd. That brash guy even took her up on the offer one night!

Our wedding night was spent at The St. Paul Hotel and our honeymoon at Madden's. One of Arlene's brothers-in-law, Frosty Jenstad, an editorial writer for the *Minneapolis Star,* was kind enough to trade cars with me that week. Arlene's sisters were evidently skeptical about my old Plymouth's ability to get us there and back. It was a nice gesture, one of many that assured me that I'd joined a close, caring family.

We started married life by living with Bertha on Pillsbury Avenue for a few months while we searched for a home of our own. We found it at 5420 Logan Avenue S., a modest, brand-new house with no garage in a neighborhood quickly developing to meet the housing demand for returning GIs. I was able to get a GI Bill mortgage with 4 percent interest rates through a mortgage company owned by the brother and father of Bud Wilkinson, who had been a star player on Bernie Bierman's championship Gopher football teams from 1934 to 1936. I don't know if that football connection helped us, but we got the house for $10,200. It sold in 2010 for $223,000.

We eventually built a garage—"we" being my neighbor Happy Peterson and me. Irwin "Happy" Peterson was a labor attorney who had about as much experience building things as I did—very little. We decided to build our garages together, as a joint project. We needed three loads of concrete for the two floors. The first load filled two-thirds of the floor of one garage. The second load was going to be the end of the first garage and the start of the second garage. It came in such a hurry that I advised the driver to take his time for the third and final load to allow us more time to smooth the wet goop into a flat floor. The third load didn't come until the day was nearly over. Happy was annoyed with me for telling the driver to slow down. I was in the doghouse, but only briefly; the driver explained that he'd had a flat tire.

I became a husband and a stepfather on the same day. Jo Anne Garniss became Jo Anne Swain—although I did not formally adopt her because doing so would end the monthly government payments to which she was entitled through age eighteen as the daughter of a deceased airman. Mac and I were determined to give her a good home—complete with younger siblings.

Over the next six and a half years we brought three children home to that little Logan Avenue house: Barbara, born May 17, 1948; Mary, January 10, 1950; and Thomas Merritt, December 7, 1953. The "Merritt" is for his Grandma Bertha; the nickname I gave Tom, "Spike," had been my dad's. Bertha was pleased with that choice and eager to watch her namesake grow up. But it wasn't to be. She died after a heart attack in May 1954 at age seventy.

CHAPTER 6

Holman Field

I ENJOYED BEING THE ACADEMIC ADVISER for the University of Minnesota Athletic Department, but as a new husband and father in 1947, I was open to another position, especially if it paid more than the modest salary I made helping athletes with their academic woes. One offer came from Les Schroeder, who had been the university's ticket manager when I worked in that office as a student employee in the late 1930s and early 1940s. He had moved across town to St. Paul's Holman Air Field and become the state commissioner of aeronautics. He said he wanted me as his administrative assistant. The job was a jack-of-all-administrative-trades sort—a little bit of budgeting, marketing, intergovernmental networking and troubleshooting, and a lot of record keeping. I'd be able to take home a $102 paycheck every two weeks. With Jo Anne's monthly Social Security check of about $20 and Arlene's monthly payment of $31.67 from Don Garniss's life insurance policy—which she receives to this day—our little household could stay in the black. I said good-bye to Goldie Gopher and revved up the '34 Plymouth for a daily drive to Holman Field, just east of downtown St. Paul.

The years after World War II brought rapid expansion of air travel in Minnesota. The Minnesota Department of Aeronautics was charged with licensing pilots, overseeing the construction of airfields, and investigating accidents. My duties included photographically documenting airplane accidents as a record for the safety review that followed them.

One day a four-passenger Navion plane took off from Holman and crashed in Owatonna, near the highway. I got the call and grabbed the office's camera, a Speed Graphic 4" × 5". It was an old-timer and not easy to operate. For each shot, the film had to be manually inserted, then pulled out of the camera's boxy body.

When I arrived that afternoon, the State Patrol was there, and a crowd had gathered. The Patrol was doing a good job cordoning off the crashed plane to keep the crowd at bay. When I identified myself, the Patrol was very helpful. They escorted me around the site as I took pictures, making me feel like a big shot. I finished, went back to the car—and realized that I hadn't taken the lens cap off.

Fortunately, my film was still unexposed. I waited until near twilight, then slunk back to the crash site. There was still enough light for me to take pictures—this time, unescorted by the State Patrol.

Les Schroeder was a tough bird, but he evidently thought enough of me to write a nice letter to the University of Minnesota Athletic Department when he wanted to hire me, explaining the reasons he wanted me to join him in state service. Through Les, I met Bill Stevenson, state's assistant commissioner of administration. We became great friends. He taught me how to lay out specifications for new state airplanes so that we had a reasonable chance to get the planes we wanted without closing the door to other bidders and running afoul of the state's procurement laws.

My stint in the aeronautics department didn't last long. It involved a good deal of travel around the state, more than a family man desired. But one day I would return to state service, and Bill and I would be on the same team.

CHAPTER 7

Ticket Man

WHEN THE UNIVERSITY OF MINNESOTA Athletic Department called me in February 1948 to offer me the ticket manager's job—Les Schroeder's old job—I jumped at it. I'd worked in that office as a student. Now, at age twenty-six, I'd be the boss, in charge of a twelve-member staff that dispensed the hottest athletic tickets in town. In 1948, Minnesota's only professional sport was the basketball Lakers, and they were a brand-new team in the infant National Basketball Association that in those years might as well have been called the Midwest League. By comparison, Gopher sports had a huge following. We sold out everything.

My philosophy was that the ticket buyer was the customer and ought to be treated right. Everybody involved in ticket transactions ought to be respectful and professional. Even if we were sold out, the ticket seekers we disappointed were prospective customers and deserved to be served with courtesy.

Being back in the ticket office brought me again into the orbit of football coach Bernie Bierman, who had known my dad. He defied the stereotype of a boisterous, attention-seeking coach. Bierman was a gentleman, quiet and something of an introvert. He had coached the Gophers in their glory days, winning five national championships between 1934 and 1941. His postwar teams were not as successful, and Bierman came in for criticism for his preference for the old-style single-wing formation rather than the modern T formation that most other teams had adopted. Single-wing lineups were deemed passé, especially by fans looking for someone to blame for the Gophers' mediocrity in the late 1940s.

The coach would occasionally come to my office during the season, sit down, and quietly visit. He wasn't there to share confidences. He just seemed to be looking for a friend—and I had the feeling that he trusted me not to share with others anything he might say. He didn't come often—just two or three times. But it was flattering for a young staffer to have a personal visit from the head coach and to be able to get to know that legendary figure as a human being.

Serious criticism of Bierman started in 1949 when the team lost to Michigan and Purdue after beating Ohio State. I was at the Michigan game. In the bus before that game, Bernie came and sat next to me and confided that he was already "really worried."

It pained me to see his career faltering in 1949, and I thought I might be of some help in giving him a graceful exit. Along with the university's swimming coach, Niels Thorpe, we got up a petition early in 1950 urging that Bernard W. Bierman should be named athletic director, succeeding Frank McCormick, who was stepping down that June. I wrote a case statement of sorts for the petition that ran to four typewritten pages and really poured it on. "Our new athletic director must be an individual highly regarded by the people of Minnesota and who possesses the ability to make friends for the University of Minnesota. Mr. Bierman's reputation among the citizens of Minnesota is unparalleled," I wrote. But collecting signatures proved more difficult than we expected. Others in the athletic department knew that Bierman's chances of getting that job were remote. The university's senior vice president for finance, W. T. Middlebrook, let it be known that the administration did not want someone of Bierman's public renown in that role. He was too big and powerful for the administration's comfort. McCormick's position went to Ike Armstrong, who became my new boss.

The criticism in 1949 was a trickle compared with the torrent that came in the 1950 season, a bad one for the Gophers. The team won only one Big Ten Conference game that season. By then, Bierman had been a collegiate head coach for thirty-one years and at the Gophers' helm for eighteen. The second-guessers in town said openly that Bierman was over the hill and had to go. They got their wish. Some of his former players met with him and told him he ought to resign rather than be fired. He took their advice. The 1950 season was his last.

I still wanted to do something for the coach. When someone suggested that a banquet be staged to honor Bierman, I eagerly agreed to be cochair of its planning committee. On February 5, 1951, in Coffman Union's ballroom, Bierman and his coaching team were given as heartfelt a tribute as that storied building had ever hosted. Nearly one thousand former players, friends, and community fans turned out to praise the best coaching record in University of Minnesota history. No other coach has come close to his achievements. I still treasure the kind personal letter I received a few days later from Bernie's wife, Clara. "Bernie and I will have happy memories all our life of the tremendous ovation and tribute afforded him that evening," she wrote.

When I took the ticket manager job, I was warned to expect that notable people would befriend me in hopes of obtaining more and better seats at the games. Don't stay too long, or you might start to believe their flattery, I was told. Some of that attention had lasting value. For example, a Dinkytown men's clothing store owner, Al Johnson, took particular interest in me and my choice of shoes. He talked me into buying a pair of Allen Edmonds shoes, a high-quality brand made in Wisconsin. "You spend much of your life on your feet, in shoes. You should have quality shoes," he told me. He convinced me to spend $20 on Scotch brogues. That was almost like buying a Cadillac. Previously, I'd never spent more than $3.30 for shoes at Thom McAn. It took some explaining to Arlene. But I've never worn anything but Allen Edmonds since, and I'm convinced that Al Johnson was right. I've never had much foot trouble. Wearing quality shoes makes a difference.

Those good shoes even helped me in a future job to make a connection with the Northwest Shoe Travelers Association. They'd shake your hand while looking at your feet to see what kind of shoes you wore. I was always well accepted because I had Allen Edmonds on. They figured this guy wears good shoes, so he must represent a good place.

Another merchant I met through ticket sales was a Minneapolis appliance dealer who gave me a very good deal on a batch of electrical appliances for our house on Logan Avenue—a stove, clothes dryer, mangle, and some other things. It was such a good deal that I couldn't refuse it. But the deal didn't include installation, and our little house wasn't wired for big power users like these. I checked into hiring an electrical contractor, but the cost was too high. I decided to learn how to wire the house myself. I bought a book for fifty cents called *Electricity Simplified.* I brought 220-volt electricity into the house for the stove and the dryer and convinced a fellow from a hardware store to come and check on my work from time to time. When I was finishing the installation of the stove, my neighbor Happy Peterson came to watch me. He accidentally bumped the back plate of the stove when I was bent down near it. The steel plate fell and cut a gash in my head severe enough to require a trip to the emergency room and some stitches. That was the only mishap associated with my venture as an electrician.

Sportswriters for the Twin Cities newspapers were particularly persistent in their requests for game tickets. I was already acquainted with one of the masters—Sid Hartman of the *Minneapolis Tribune.* Sid and I are nearly the same age. We both grew up in Minneapolis, on opposite sides of town. He lived on the North Side, in what was then a Jewish and African American enclave, and didn't have an easy start in life. His father was an alcoholic, leaving his wife and four children with depleted resources. Even as a kid, Sid compensated by working hard, first by delivering newspapers, then as a gofer at the old *Minneapolis Times,* an afternoon paper. Through sheer persistence, he struck up a friendship with Dick Cullum, the *Times's* sports editor. Cullum became a second father to Sid and gave him a chance to break into sports reporting and editing. He wasn't a great writer, but no reporter was more dogged, on any beat. When the *Times* folded in 1948, Sid and Dick were both snapped up by the *Minneapolis Tribune's* sports editor Charlie Johnson.

I met Sid while I was the athletic department's academic adviser and he was a cub reporter for the *Times.* We weren't exactly in sync from the start. I was trying to keep the players studying; Sid was offering them distraction and temptation. His reporting technique was to cozy up to players, socialize with them, do them favors such as loaning a car and/or cash for a date, then badger them to reveal more than they should about team matters. Marsh Ryman was my boss at the time; he went on to be athletic director for the university in the 1960s. Bernie Bierman was never enamored of sportswriters, and some of that attitude rubbed off on Ryman. At one point, Marsh was angry enough at Sid's interference with players' lives to talk about physically deterring him from contacting them. I once found myself reassuring Bierman that though Sid was loud and rambunctious, he was basically harmless.

By the time I was ticket manager, Sid was the go-to guy for the older sportswriters at the *Tribune*. They sent him to campus to bring back scoops they could use. When they wanted special tickets, they'd send Sid to me. Knowing on whose behalf he was asking, I sought to accommodate his requests. I thought that only made sense. Good relations with the city's leading newspaper were in the university's best interests, I reasoned. Sid didn't exactly come hat in hand to my office. He'd swoop in with a booming voice and bark his requests. But I saw past his brash manner and came to admire a guy with an extraordinary work ethic and loyalty to his family, employers, sources, and the state of Minnesota. I became one of Sid's many "close personal friends," a label he put on hundreds of people through the years on his WCCO radio broadcasts. In our case, the description rang true.

The same could not be said about Sid's relationship with Marsh Ryman, however. Ryman spent more than forty years associated with Gopher athletics as a star hockey player, coach, ticket manager, business manager, and athletic director. When he was inducted into the National Association of College Athletic Directors' Hall of Fame in 1978, I thought he deserved to be one of Sid's featured personalities on his WCCO radio spot, *Today's Sports Hero*. I said as much in a letter to Sid in June 1978. No response. I decided I wasn't going to take silence for an answer. My notes indicate that I called Sid nineteen times between 1978 and 1985 to ask him to give Ryman some recognition. But Sid proved he could outlast me. Marsh Ryman died in 1992, having never been a Sid Hartman "sports hero."

One conversation I had with Sid in the mid-1950s might have been fateful for local sports history. Sid had helped bring the Minneapolis Lakers into being in 1947, organizing local investors to buy a failing National Basketball League franchise in Detroit and move that team here. (The notion of conflict of interest had not yet dawned on newspaper sports journalists.) Max Winter was the team's general manager, but Sid ran player recruitment and was always in the room when major decisions were made.

The Lakers had extraordinary success on the basketball court, winning six national championships between 1948 and 1960. The team was also instrumental in spurring the merger of the National Basketball League and the Basketball Association of America to form today's NBA. But winning didn't assure financial stability. The team played at the Minneapolis Armory and the Minneapolis Auditorium, both lousy venues for basketball. Ultimately, their audience began to fade.

I was working for the St. Paul convention bureau at the time. It occurred to me that the name "Minneapolis" wasn't helping the Lakers draw fans from St. Paul. "You need to change the name from the Minneapolis Lakers to the Minnesota Lakers," I told Sid. "You need to get it broadened out." He pooh-poohed my idea.

In 1960—when Sid was again much involved in recruiting professional teams to Minnesota—the Lakers left for Los Angeles. The teams he helped snare were named the Minnesota Twins and the Minnesota Vikings. Every professional team since—the Timberwolves, the Wild, the Kicks—has used the name Minnesota, not Minneapolis.

Halsey Hall was also one of my buddies. Hall would become best known as the radio voice of Minnesota Twins baseball after that team's arrival in 1961. But he had been broadcasting Gopher football games before that and had been a popular sportswriter for both Minneapolis and St. Paul newspapers since the 1920s. He was a character, known for his love of cigars, Scotch whiskey, and a good story, preferably told by him. While broadcasting football games, he'd get so carried away with his stories and his descriptions of the plays that he'd sometimes forget to report where the ball was. "Holy cow!" he'd say after a touchdown. When he started using that exclamation after the Twins hit a home run, it stuck, and was "borrowed" by Harry Caray in Chicago. Caray made a trademark of the line he stole from Halsey Hall.

The best memory I have of Halsey was on a Gopher football trip to Seattle via train in 1950. Halsey famously hated flying but enjoyed the leisure (and refreshment) that train travel afforded. It took us two days to get to Seattle, or close to it, and we played gin rummy much of the time. Halsey was my partner against Charlie

Johnson and another broadcaster, Rollie Johnson from WTCN Radio. Halsey enjoyed his drinks, so much that I feared that I was at a disadvantage with Halsey as my partner. But he held up well and kept us laughing. He always did.

My relationship with the local sportswriters was a two-way street. When I needed their help at the start of the 1950–51 basketball season, they were there for me. The Gophers' basketball home then and now was the Minnesota Field House, now known as Williams Arena. Built in 1927–28, it came up for major renovation and expansion in the summer and fall of 1950. I was all for the changes, so much so that I put together some statistics documenting the need for more space. I made bold to offer the numbers to Charlie Johnson, the *Tribune*'s sports editor, in reply to his letter to me requesting that his seats for the coming football season be moved slightly higher in the stadium. Charlie had been a big advocate of the university adding a second deck to Memorial Stadium. Among other things, such an addition would improve the press box and add an elevator, sparing Charlie the need to climb sixty-two steps in the stadium to get there. Frank McCormick, the athletic director, went so far as to look into the idea. But he concluded that it would be much too costly. The Field House renovation looked more doable, and I helped sell it to Charlie.

As often happens, the project ran behind schedule. A strike that year in the steel industry delayed the installation of structural beams essential to the project. I was obliged to start selling tickets for the new season without knowing precisely how many seats would be available for use at each game. The possibilities ranged from 4,500 to 20,000. The *Minneapolis Star*'s Dick Gordon helped me cool the ire of unhappy basketball fans with a sympathetic story. "If you think things are tough, bend an ear to the heartbreak of Thomas Swain, athletic ticket manager at the University of Minnesota," began a story published on November 24 about the season that would open on December 3. "Tom has drawn up so many different seating blueprints that his own face is a blueprint—of despair."

Athletic director Frank McCormick made a public boast that the remodeled arena would seat 20,000, then told me to work with the building's designers to make sure his vow was kept. When the renovations were complete, the arena would indeed seat 20,000—if you crammed as many bodies as possible into bench seats and compelled them to sit sidesaddle. Today, Williams Arena has 14,000 seats again, the same number we had before the renovation.

I became close to some of the athletes. In those years, players were allotted a certain number of free tickets that they could use as they wished. I took good care of the players and made sure their tickets were for good seats. Each year of play earned players more tickets. By the time they were seniors, they received six free and six priority tickets per game. The latter were excellent seats at a discounted price. These were for sell-out games, mind you—those tickets were valuable commodities. The more entrepreneurial players sold their tickets for handsome prices. More than one player told me that I had enabled them to get through their college careers with a measure of financial comfort that they would have otherwise lacked.

In December 1950—just as plans were being set for the banquet saluting Bernie Bierman—I was approached with a job offer. The board of the Convention and Visitors Bureau of the St. Paul Association of Commerce (today it is the Chamber of Commerce) was chaired by a big Gopher sports fan, Bill Haman. He was the sales manager for Schmidt Brewing Co., then a fixture west of downtown St. Paul. He approached me when the bureau's top staff job, its manager, became vacant and encouraged me to apply. I was mindful of the advice I'd heard in 1948: if I stayed in the ticket manager's job more than three years, the flattery would go to my head. My counterpart at Purdue University, C. S. Doan, told me in a letter that a person who stays too long in a Division I ticket manager's job is "either numb or dumb." I also worried that the university job wouldn't lead to advancement—something that was on my mind in 1950 as the father of three small children in a still-growing family. The convention bureau seemed like a springboard to other things, and it paid more. "I owe it to both my family and myself to attempt to improve upon my status," I wrote to Ike Armstrong, the new athletic director.

"I am still and probably always will be very much wrapped up in the interests of the University of Minnesota," my letter ended. Those were prescient words.

CHAPTER 8

Come to St. Paul

Taking a job in st. paul wasn't exactly a move to a foreign land. But one hundred years of archrivalry and demographic differences resulted in the Twin Cities being quite distinct from one another in the 1950s. My new job as St. Paul Association of Commerce's Convention Bureau manager didn't require me to move to St. Paul. In fact, my counterpart in Minneapolis, Julius Perlt, lived in St. Paul. "You're taking the heat off me to move, Tom," he told me after learning I lived in south Minneapolis.

But after the birth of our son Tom in December 1953, we needed a bigger house. I pressed the case with Arlene that it should be in St. Paul, to shorten my commute and tie me more closely to my professional community. You'd think I was asking her to move to Libya or Afghanistan. It soothed her somewhat that the three-story house we found at 2270 Riverwood Place was near the city's western edge and equidistant to the two downtowns. Better still, it was situated in one of the few St. Paul telephone exchanges in which calls to Minneapolis were free. In most of St. Paul in the 1950s, a call to Minneapolis cost ten cents. Arlene could call her sisters in Minneapolis free of charge from MI-3145, for which we were both grateful. In short order, Arlene was sold on St. Paul.

The rivalry between St. Paul and Minneapolis always seemed somewhat laughable—in Minneapolis. In St. Paul, I discovered, the competition was keenly felt. St. Paulites considered being overshadowed by a larger and more affluent neighbor a real economic threat. Minneapolis was the name that was known around the world. St. Paul was the older city, the capital city, and the proud home of prestigious private colleges, 3M, and the Great Northern and Northern Pacific railroads. But it was too often an afterthought as a destination for tourism, conventions, and business investment.

My job was to change that, at least where conventions and tourism were concerned.

I got off to an inauspicious start on March 1, 1951. I parked my car on a surface lot at the corner of Cedar Street and Kellogg Boulevard. At the day's end, my car wouldn't start. I didn't know my way around, and when I asked for help from the fellows who ran the lot, they brushed me off. "That's your problem," they said. Those fellows eventually became my friends, and I parked in their lot for more than five years. But I wouldn't recommend them for the Welcome Wagon.

My office mate in our corner office in the St. Paul Athletic Club was Fran Kaar, who was responsible for the relationships between the Association of Commerce and wholesalers. He and I often lamented that journalists would say or write that the State Fair was in Minneapolis. In fact, it straddles the border between St. Paul and Falcon Heights. Often, the local radio station with multistate reach, WCCO, would identify its home base as Minneapolis and never mention St. Paul. Fran and I came up with a way for St. Paul people to end that omission. We organized about thirty-five or forty willing guys into the Wambuts, an acronym for "We Ain't Mad—But!" We printed and distributed business cards with our logo, a feathered Indian reaching out to a white-skinned hand with a peace pipe and carrying a sharp tomahawk behind his back. That logo was terribly racially insensitive and would never pass muster today, but in the early 1950s, it was in keeping with the attitudes of that time.

The back of the card read: "Greetings from the Wambuts. Unintentionally, we trust, you have committed a grievous, lamentable error against the historic and fair city of ST. PAUL. Assuming you will be more accurate in the future, we're offering this puff on our pipe of peace. But remember, our tomahawk is razor-keen, and the Wambuts are watching you." The idea was that whenever one of our group encountered a public omission or slight toward St. Paul, he'd give or send the perpetrator a card and then alert me. I was the group's secretary—they called me the Super Chief. (I know, that sounds bad today.) I would inform the rest of the group, all of whom had pledged to descend on the perpetrator with more cards. Within a few days, the hapless soul or souls who had slighted

St. Paul would be inundated with thirty or forty cards, either mailed or hand delivered. It was that effort that got Twin Cities TV and radio stations to rotate the city names as they announced their call letters and location. One hour it would be "This is WCCO, Minneapolis and St. Paul" and the next it would be "WCCO, St. Paul and Minneapolis."

St. Paul banks were independent from the ones in Minneapolis in those years. Bankers were especially sensitive to rivalry with their Minneapolis counterparts. Wally Boss was senior vice president of the First National Bank of St. Paul. (Wally's son Andy was also a banker, the president of St. Anthony Park Bank, and like his dad, a real force for civic good.) Wally inspired the rest of us Wambuts with his response aboard a Capital Airlines flight to the Twin Cities. When the flight attendant announced, "This is flight such-and-so from New York to Minneapolis," Wally jumped out of his seat and hollered, "I'm on the wrong plane!" He loudly told her that his destination was St. Paul, not Minneapolis. He memorably made his point with her and everyone else on board.

The Wambuts experience showed me that St. Paul business leaders were quite willing to pitch in on projects to promote the city. I sought out local members of national trade or industrial associations and asked them to convince those national groups to bring their conventions to St. Paul. I'd help with the sales pitch, traveling as needed, and make sure our members were armed with glossy information about St. Paul. We'd brag about the hotels in the city, most of which are gone today—the Lowry, the Ryan, the St. Clair, the St. Francis, the Capri, the Frederick, Lakes & Pine Motel. Only The St. Paul Hotel, the city's finest then and now, is still standing. Admittedly, aside from The St. Paul, we didn't have a strong hand to play—not in comparison with the Leamington, Curtis, Nicollet, and Radisson in Minneapolis. But we offered affordability, walkability, and the small-city charm that some groups preferred.

One such was the Farmers Union Grain Terminal Association. Its annual meeting each December was easy to land. Its long-time general manager, M. W. Thatcher, wanted nothing to do with the grain-trading people in Minneapolis—even though one of his great friends and political allies was the former mayor of Minneapolis,

U.S. Sen. Hubert Humphrey. Thatcher made quite a show of his annual "state of the union" address in the theater section of the St. Paul Auditorium (now the Roy Wilkins Auditorium). After his oration, he'd retire to a dressing room and hold court for a select few friends. When he invited me, I was advised that I should consider the invitation a great honor.

The St. Paul Association of Commerce's board leaders in those days were very conservative, politically speaking. The dominant figures were Bill Moscrip, a large-scale breeder of Holstein Friesian cattle, and Norris Carnes of the Central Livestock Association. They didn't exactly project an image of urban vitality. But fortunately the convention bureau had its own board, recruited at my discretion, its own fund-raising operation, and control of its own budget. That gave me a good deal of latitude to find an answer to a question I mulled in an attempt to sell St. Paul as a tourism and convention destination: What's our attraction? What's here to see that's worth turning off the highway? What could persuade tourists heading to northern Minnesota to stop in St. Paul, not Minneapolis? Greensburg, Kansas—population 1,723—was luring 80,000 tourists per year from U.S. Highway 54 with a come-on for the "largest hand-dug well in the world." What did St. Paul have that was the world's largest?

The answer we hit on in 1953 was only a few blocks away, in the St. Paul City Hall / Ramsey County Courthouse lobby. It was the magnificent Mexican white onyx sculpture then called the *Indian God of Peace,* today known as the *Vision of Peace.* It was carved as a memorial to Minnesota's World War I dead by Swedish sculptor Carl Milles, who drew his inspiration from a Native American ceremony he witnessed in Oklahoma. It depicts a mythical figure rising out of the smoke of a peace pipe ceremony being conducted by five men sitting council-style around a fire. It is nearly three stories tall, weighs 60 tons, and slowly rotates 132 degrees—66 degrees to the left, then 66 degrees to the right. That pivot inspired one of its somewhat unfortunate nicknames, Whirling Joe. The locals also called it Onyx John, and not with much respect. The sculpture wasn't new; it had been presiding over the city hall lobby without much notice since 1936. No matter. We could introduce Whirling

Joe as "the world's tallest Indian," which was well worth seeing—especially if sufficiently promoted by billboards on U.S. Highways 10 and 12, then the major arteries for tourists from Chicago heading each summer to Minnesota's northern lake resorts.

The idea was presented to our board in April 1953, complete with some suggestions for give-away bait. Free parking for vehicles bearing out-of-state licenses was one idea. Free fishing licenses, sponsored by local merchants, was another. We could set up a tourism information booth in the lobby near our statue, directing tourists to the Capitol, Como Park Zoo, or Keller Golf Course. We even proposed a colored stripe down the middle of some streets to mark the way for directionally challenged tourists. There would be no mention of the lakes, waterfalls, parks, and museums in Brand X city next door. People could figure that out for themselves.

The idea was a hit. The *St. Paul Pioneer Press* and its afternoon counterpart, the *St. Paul Dispatch,* were all in to help with promotion. My crucial partner was Walter Broich, president of the Naegele Advertising Company—the billboard people. They designed a billboard featuring a cutout of the sculpture and the St. Paul skyline and helped us decide where best to use them. Our role was to convince local merchants to sponsor the signs. They could have their own messages on the billboards between Labor Day and June 15, but for two and a half months each summer, the individual merchants' messages were replaced by a series of slogans promoting "St. Paul's Indian."

It wasn't hard to sell the signs—not when we explained that tourism was already the state's third-largest industry and that St. Paul stood to capture more of the $265 million tourists spent in Minnesota per year in the early 1950s. Our initial goal was to sell 40 billboards. The response was so good that we wound up with 134 billboards the first year, 1955, and more for several years after.

Better still, the promotion worked. In its first six weeks, 10,000 tourists registered at the new information desk at City Hall, a majority of them saying they came because of the highway signs. Many more came without registering. In the summer of 1957, the tally was up to 65,000. A ceremony on August 30, 1955, rededicated the statue, involving political leaders and Ojibwe Chief Ay-co-ge-shig from Milaca, Minnesota, who rode horseback for three days to get there. That feat even attracted coverage in the Minneapolis newspapers. At random, we chose the James Lynch family of Glenview, Illinois, as our Minnesota Tourist Family of 1955 and arranged for them to meet Governor Orville Freeman as part of their stay in St. Paul. That, too, got headlines.

I got some nice notice as a result. The headline of a feature article in the September 1955 edition of *The Jay Scene,* the magazine of the St. Paul Junior Chamber of Commerce, was "Swain Finds an Indian." "The success of the program is living tribute to the man in whose brain the seedling was nurtured and brought to full blossom—Tom Swain," the article said. Of course, the local Jaycees had reason to say nice things about me in 1955. I was a chapter vice president that year.

CHAPTER 9

A Royal Kiss

THE ST. PAUL JAYCEES brought me in contact with Peter Popovich, a bright, gregarious attorney and state legislator. A native of Crosby and Chisholm on Minnesota's Iron Range, Popovich was just seven months older than I was. He would go on to be the founding chief judge of the Minnesota Court of Appeals and chief justice of the Minnesota Supreme Court. In the 1950s, he was an ambitious municipal-bond lawyer with a fun-loving nature unspoiled by a hardscrabble youth and a frightening battle with polio as a young adult. It also partially masked his serious-minded interest in public policy and state history. Popovich had worked his way through law school by serving on the staff of the state's Territorial Centennial Commission in 1949. The Peterson and Popovich law office was across the street from the convention bureau, which afforded a chance for our acquaintance through the Jaycees to blossom into friendship.

In 1955, while I was busy selling conventions, Popovich was at work in the Minnesota House as the chief sponsor of legislation initiating the celebration of Minnesota's statehood centennial in 1958. His bill authorized the creation of a planning commission, to consist of five state senators, five representatives, and five gubernatorial appointees, and the hiring of an executive director to create and execute a plan for a year of observances. The bill passed, the commission convened, and Popovich was elected its chair. He asked me to apply for the executive director's job.

My initial response: "I don't think my politics are right." Popovich was a DFLer, the governor was a DFLer, and I presumed they wanted another DFLer for the top staff job. I hadn't been involved in politics, but I considered myself a Republican. I wasn't a straight-ticket guy. For example, I preferred Humphrey over Republican

Senator Joe Ball in 1948. But I preferred Thomas Dewey to Harry Truman for president in 1948, and Ike over Adlai both times, in 1952 and 1956.

But Popovich assured me that my proclivities at the polls were no disqualification for a job that he knew would be a big organizational challenge. It meant starting something from scratch, engaging hundreds of volunteers, and operating with a tight budget. The challenge appealed to me as well as the chance to accomplish some good in the name of public service. It was the sort of thing I would be attracted to throughout my professional life. In addition, I liked Popovich and relished the chance to work with him for a few years. I was offered the job and accepted it. I was to start work on March 1, 1956.

Shortly before I started, the Centennial Commission was saddled with a delicate complication of Popovich's making.

In late January 1956, the St. Paul Association of Commerce was hosting its annual dinner at The St. Paul Hotel in conjunction with the St. Paul Winter Carnival. Even though the Legislature did not meet in 1956, legislators and the governor were our invited guests. The event began with a reception that I attended, thinking I might mingle with the lawmakers whose support the centennial project would soon require. I didn't stay for dinner. As I was leaving, I ran into Governor Orville and First Lady Jane Freeman. I stuck around just long enough to help them check their coats and usher them to their places at the head table in the banquet hall. Freeman was to be among the featured speakers. Thinking all was well, I left for an evening with my family.

The next morning, I had a call from my friend Paul Hagstrum of Hagstrum Bros. Clothing. He was chair of the Winter Carnival board of directors that year. "Did you hear what happened? Vulcanus Rex and his crew came in. They swept around and closed in on Jane Freeman. When they separated and left, Jane and the governor, obviously very distraught, got up and left before the governor gave his speech."

I moaned in dismay. The Vulcan Krewe was a notorious part of Winter Carnival tradition. Lore has it that Vulcanus Rex, the King of Fire, must battle each year for control of St. Paul with King

Boreas, the King of the Winds. Rex and his men lived together in a hotel during the run of the carnival, often enjoying a goodly quantity of strong liquid refreshment, and swooped around town dressed in red capes. They wore masks and greasepaint makeup to hide their identities. Their schtick included "marking" with greasepaint the faces of women they encountered. Smears of greasepaint were administered via cheek-to-cheek contact and sometimes something more intimate.

The thought that pretty, proper Jane Freeman had been publicly "marked" by these jokers at a St. Paul Association of Commerce event was bad enough. But there was more.

"Do you know who Vulcanus Rex is this year?" Paul asked.

"No," I said, "and I don't care."

"You should," Paul countered. "He's your new boss."

Popovich was that year's Vulcanus Rex. In full regalia, he had approached the head table and forced what in Winter Carnival lingo is called "a royal kiss" on the first lady of Minnesota. A royal kiss is no mere peck on the cheek. This one was said to be quite aggressive and prolonged. And Orv Freeman was nothing if not a protective husband.

The enmity of the governor would be a big setback to our effort to win funding from the 1957 Legislature for the centennial observance, I thought. I called Popovich and told him that I wouldn't take the executive director's job unless he was willing to meet with Freeman and apologize. Popovich wasn't eager to do so; he considered his action merely good fun. But I pressed him, and he reluctantly agreed that if Freeman would see him, he would apologize.

Hagstrum and I paid a call on the governor to convey Popovich's desire to meet him and apologize. It was the shortest meeting with a politician that I ever attended. "You tell that SOB that if he comes here, I'll kill him!" Freeman said. Then he took my elbow with a grip like a vise and propelled me out the door.

I thought it over and decided not to renege on my commitment to take the job. Popovich had satisfied my condition by being willing to apologize. The governor's unwillingness to receive the apology was out of our hands.

Freeman wasn't through punishing us. The commission office

was supposed to be in the Veterans Services Building on the south side of the Capitol mall. Art Naftalin, the commissioner of administration (today it's management and budget), a future Minneapolis mayor and Freeman's good friend, evicted us with no explanation. We were convinced that it happened at Freeman's direction. We turned that challenge to our advantage by finding an office at Prior and University Avenues in St. Paul and persuading the U.S. Post Office to change its address from 1960-something to "1958 University." That good idea came from the fertile mind of Don Padilla, a talented publicist whom we hired as director of publicity for the centennial.

The 1957 Legislature came up with an additional $1 million for our office, a generous sum in those days. To my relief, Freeman signed the bill. However, he did not speak to Popovich all that session, the last before the yearlong celebration began. Plans were coming together nicely as that year progressed. By December— nearly two years after the dastardly "marking" episode—I decided to call on Freeman one more time to broach the subject of his relationship with Popovich.

"Next year is going to be big for Minnesota and big for you," I told the governor. "You and Representative Popovich are going to be on the same platform frequently. If the feelings that you have toward him are transparent, it will become a topic for comment."

"You're right," Freeman responded. "I'll behave myself. But I still hate that SOB with an intensity I can't describe!"

A few days later, at a 1957 year-end ceremony at the Capitol rotunda, Popovich formally presented a specially designed centennial flag to Freeman. Freeman was as good as his word. His stony face revealed no emotion. A photograph published the next day in the *Minneapolis Tribune* shows a bugler in Civil War garb performing while Freeman and Popovich sat in opposite corners behind him, about thirty feet apart. The significance of that wide gap was undoubtedly lost on newspaper readers other than me.

A SEQUEL TO MY CONNECTION to the Vulcan Krewe occurred many years later. In 2005, the Vulcan king and his gang were charged in both criminal and civil court with sexual harassment of three

St. Paul waitresses while attempting to force garters onto their legs. The Winter Carnival board decided that they'd had enough. The Krewe needed reformation, they said, and they asked me to chair a blue-ribbon committee to recommend changes. I was reluctant until I thought, well, somebody has to do it. I saw to it that the task force included a real cross-section of the community, including strong women such as former state finance commissioner Pam Wheelock, then an executive with the Minnesota Wild hockey team.

Many observers thought we would recommend that the Vulcans be disrobed and disbanded. Instead, we came up with a batch of recommendations, including one that a *Star Tribune* editorial called "powerful (and) elegant in its simplicity." No more would Vulcans be anonymous or go by character pseudonyms such as "Baron Hot Sparkus" and "Grand Duke Fertilious." They would be required to put their real names on name tags prominently worn with their Vulcan Krewe costumes. Krewe members are successful middle-aged men who can ill afford to sully their good names with the kind of misconduct that landed the 2005 Krewe on the city's police blotter. In addition, Vulcans were forbidden to attempt to put garters, pins, or jewelry on women or to consume alcohol while in costume. (They had already been directed in the 1970s to stop forcing kisses on unwilling women.) Eight carnivals later, it appears that the changes our task force recommended are working.

Floyd and Judy at the Centennial

A SKING THE 1957 LEGISLATURE for $1.7 million was "the apogee of optimism," according to *Minneapolis Star* and *Tribune* editor Bill Steven, whom Don Padilla and I courted in hopes of securing favorable coverage of our efforts. Steven was right. The total state appropriation earmarked for the Centennial Commission was $1.1 million. That sounds meager today, but it was enough for us to function.

The 1955 legislation establishing the commission came with very little money—barely enough to hire me. But that bill contained a couple of specific directives concerning statues, which evidently were on legislators' minds that year. Congress had given each state the opportunity to place two statues in the U.S. Capitol, one in Statuary Hall, the other elsewhere in the building. Minnesota's man in Statuary Hall was Henry Rice, a nineteenth-century fur trader and politician who helped shepherd the statehood bill through Congress in the 1850s and then became the state's first U.S. senator.

The 1955 bill directed that the second statue in the nation's Capitol should depict Maria Sanford, the first female professor at the University of Minnesota and for twenty-nine years a popular teacher of literature, rhetoric, and art history. A special committee was established for that project, headed by state Sen. Elmer L. Andersen, who represented the northwestern corner of the city of St. Paul. Elmer was also a businessman, the owner and CEO of H. B. Fuller Co., and very involved in community affairs. He had to be very busy. Yet I observed that he took the statue assignment very seriously. He worked hard to ensure a quality product and a favorable location in the Capitol for Maria. When it was installed, Elmer and I went to Washington together for the ceremony and became better acquainted. I learned later that he had noticed my work too.

64

The 1955 Legislature also wanted a statue of former governor Floyd B. Olson to be placed on the state Capitol grounds and dedicated as part of the centennial observance. Olson had nothing to do with securing statehood for Minnesota. He came along much later, as an anticorruption Hennepin County attorney in the 1920s and the state's first Farmer-Labor Party governor in the 1930s. As governor, he was a champion for working people, small farmers, and public education. He died in office in 1936, assuring that he would be remembered as a tragic hero who might have done greater things had stomach cancer not ended his life at age forty-four. The Legislature's order to place a statue of Olson across the street from the State Office Building shows that nineteen years after his death, he was still on Minnesotans' minds.

Fulfilling that order fell to the Centennial Commission, which meant to a committee, which meant to me. I wanted to proceed as economically as possible. It came to my attention that Amerigo "Babe" Brioschi, a St. Paul sculptor, and his father Carlo had produced the statue of Olson that was erected in about 1940 in Minneapolis, at the corner of Penn and Sixth Avenues N., the latter of which thereafter was known as Olson Memorial Highway. Brioschi came to see me and said, "Tom, I can do this for you at a pretty low cost. I've kept the molds from the statue in Minneapolis. It's got his right arm up. I'll just switch the arms so your statue will be different. It'll have the left arm up." He quoted a good price. I said, "You're on."

When the time came to dedicate the statue in 1958, the statue's committee asked me to contact Governor Olson's widow and daughter to invite them to attend the ceremony. Ada Krejci Olson, who married the future governor in 1917, had moved to Brainerd in 1951; their daughter Patricia was their only child and had been a high school classmate of mine. I called her to extend the invitation. Patty wasn't very enthusiastic. The relationship between Olson and his family had been somewhat strained, I learned. But she finally said, "If it's important, we'll come."

I had one more question for her: "What was Floyd's favorite song?" The committee wanted to include it in the program. Patty allowed that she didn't know and didn't care. That ended the conversation.

At the next committee meeting, a fellow from the musician's union was in attendance. When I reported that I didn't have an answer to the favorite-song question, he piped up: "Everybody knows Floyd B. Olson's favorite song. It was 'God Bless America.'" That was assurance enough for us. "God Bless America" would be a prominent part of the program.

Befitting a Farmer-Labor Party leader, the ceremony was scheduled for Labor Day. On the Sunday morning of Labor Day weekend, I was in the office when our pageant director, Bob Snook, came in, ashen-faced.

"What's the matter?" I asked.

"Do you know when 'God Bless America' was written?" Snook asked, then answered his own question. "It was in 1938—two years after Floyd died!"

I let that fact sink in for a moment, then said, "It's too late now to change the program. We're going ahead with it." (Actually, Irving Berlin had written the song in 1918 but set it aside until 1938, when Kate Smith sang it for the first time on her radio show.)

I kept my fingers crossed at that ceremony. Would somebody notice the similarity between the new Floyd statue and the older one in Minneapolis? Would someone question our claim that "God Bless America" was Olson's favorite song? To my relief, nobody did.

ONE OF THE GREAT MOVES we made early in the centennial's planning was to hire Don Padilla to do publicity. A native of Iowa and a former boxer, Don had worked on the air at WTCN (now KARE) TV and had been a news director at WCCO-TV before he accepted our job offer in 1956. He went on to found one of the top public relations firms in the Twin Cities, Padilla & Speer (now Padilla Speer Beardsley) with Dave Speer, who was publicity director for the St. Paul Winter Carnival during our centennial project.

Don was a high-energy, public-spirited guy who was full of ideas. We agreed that the centennial was a fine opportunity for Minnesotans to toot their own horns and tell the rest of the country that this is a great place. Self-promotion doesn't come naturally to a lot of Minnesotans. There's a lot of truth to the stereotypes about Minnesota Nice and Scandinavian reserve. We wanted to invite them to overcome their reluctance to brag—and along the way, convince themselves to better appreciate Minnesota.

We concluded that there ought to be a centennial committee in every county. Hennepin and Ramsey did it differently, but we were able to establish coordinating committees in eighty-four of the eighty-seven counties. We hired two fellows, Bill Stohr and Art Nyhus, as liaisons to these committees, which consisted entirely of volunteers. Before a county formed its committee, we'd pay a visit to explain to potential committee members the opportunity the centennial celebration afforded for promoting their county and region. That meant a lot of travel. We established a routine: four county visits per week, two per day—one at noon, one at night, with one overnight away from home. We'd try to visit contiguous counties each week to keep travel time and cost down. Local legislators would be invited to emcee the meetings, which typically involved thirty or forty people.

This was more frequent public speaking than my previous jobs required, and it taught me to deal with a certain amount of adversity. For example, in Alexandria, just as I started speaking, the local Rotary Club meeting at the same restaurant in an adjacent room started loudly singing "The Star Spangled Banner." I didn't quite know what to do. I hope I did the appropriate thing—I stopped until they were finished. Shortly after I resumed, a waitress came into the room and attempted to collect the per-person fee for the lunch we'd been served. Some of those in attendance were hard of hearing. My message was interrupted by her repeated litany, "Dollar and a half! Dollar and a half!" When that distraction ended, I heard wheezing nearby. The state senator who had introduced me had a breathing problem. I thought he was having a heart attack and stopped again. Fortunately, his condition wasn't that serious. But my speech was in disarray.

It was nothing, though, compared with what happened that night. We were in Glenwood, in Pope County. State Rep. Delbert Anderson was supposed to introduce me, but he begged off to attend a Flying Farmers gathering in Duluth. The head of the county historical society introduced me instead. He was an older fellow and an impatient sort. We usually called our evening meetings for 7:30

and got started about 7:45, to give latecomers a chance to get settled. That didn't suit this chap. At 7:32 he asked, "When are we going to get started?"

I told him we usually begin at 7:45.

Five minutes later, he told me, "We have to get under way."

His introduction was nothing special. "There are a couple of guys from headquarters here to talk to us," he told the group.

I got started with my remarks, which included a few lame jokes to warm up the crowd. I'd been speaking for about five minutes when the fellow who introduced me, now sitting in the front row, raised his hand. "You've told a couple of jokes. It's getting late," he said. "When are you going to quit?"

I kept going. Five minutes later, he raised his hand again.

"Really, it's getting late," he said.

If Representative Anderson, whom I knew, had been there, I would have turned to him for counsel about whether to continue. But I didn't have a friend in the room, other than my staff member Bill. I saw heads in the audience nodding yes and no, and couldn't discern their meaning. So I did something that may have been unprecedented in public speaking. I asked for a vote on whether I should continue or cease. Mercifully, they voted I should continue. I proceeded with my talk; Bill followed with his portion of the program. There were so many questions, including some from our impatient host, that we were there until nearly 11:00 P.M.

PLANNING FOR THE CENTENNIAL OBSERVANCE involved many statewide committees coordinated by our office, which eventually grew to twenty-six salaried employees. We put the centennial label on everything we could think of, including things that would have happened anyway, regardless of the state's one-hundredth birthday. The St. Paul Winter Carnival, the Minneapolis Aquatennial, the State Fair—all had a centennial theme in 1958. All told, by one estimate, 11,000 people participated in centennial event planning, and upward of 900,000 of the state's 3 million people participated in centennial events. People from all walks and stations of life got involved. For example, Grace Bliss Dayton—the grandmother of our current governor, Mark Dayton—and Vivian Weyerhaeuser, the granddaughter-in-law of the founder of the Weyerhaeuser timber company, headed our women's committee. We had just about every kind of event you can imagine—a treasure hunt, a youth essay contest, a Pony Express relay, an outdoor poetry festival, a commemorative stamp dedication, a festival of nations, and on and on. There was even a centennial violin-making contest.

Our sports committee was particularly active. Their big idea was to establish the Minnesota Sports Hall of Fame. The jointly owned *Minneapolis Star* and *Minneapolis Tribune* agreed to sponsor the Hall of Fame exhibit, which eventually was housed in the recently demolished Metrodome. I expect to see it reappear at the new Minnesota Vikings stadium.

That committee also decided to try to lure the NCAA hockey championship tournament from Colorado Springs, Colorado, to Minnesota in 1958. This is "the state of hockey," after all. But University of Minnesota hockey coach John Mariucci wasn't keen on our idea. He liked having a professional excuse to go to Colorado Springs and stay at the Broadmoor Hotel each year. But Marsh Ryman, the university Athletic Department's business manager and assistant hockey coach, loved the idea. He checked with a few other hockey coaches around the country, and they agreed that it would be good if the tournament's location shifted from year to year, building more fan interest in the sport.

The 1957 meeting of the nation's hockey coaches was in Boston. Marsh, Mariucci, and I were there. Mariucci's assignment at a morning meeting was to present the proposal that the hockey tournament be moved to Minnesota the following year. The time for the meeting came, and there was no Mariucci. Ryman went to the front desk and got a key. I went with Marsh to Mariucci's room. We found him still in bed. I stayed in the deep background to see what would ensue. Marsh was a tough guy, and he wasn't going to put up with Mariucci's excuses. "Get your butt out of bed and get going!" Ryman yelled. He did, and the proposal prevailed. The 1958 tournament came to Minnesota, and it has rotated every year since.

ONE OF THE THINGS we thought we needed in the early going was a centennial emblem. Naturally, that meant we needed an emblem committee. That committee came in for what I believe was more than its share of criticism, some of it lingering to this day. The committee recommended a design. The full commission suggested some changes, the committee came back with a final product, and the commission unanimously approved the final version. It featured the back-to-back profiles of a man and a woman towering over small symbols of Minnesota's leading industries—agriculture, timber, manufacturing, and shipping. On the left side of the array of industrial symbols was a silo. To balance its height on the right side, the artist, Will Schaeffer of St. Louis Park, placed what could be seen as a simple power line or telephone pole—or a Christian cross.

We unveiled the design to the public in October 1956 and sent it to newspapers around the state. A few days later, we heard from Sam Scheiner, the executive director of the Minnesota Jewish Council. "This is a Christian cross, and that's unacceptable," he told me. It excluded non-Christian Minnesotans from the centennial observance. Scheiner's message was the start of an awful furor. One of the people on the commission was Aaron Litman, the Jewish publisher of the White Bear Press newspaper. He had approved the design and said it was outstanding. If he or any of us had understood the symbol to be a Christian cross, we wouldn't have proceeded.

I ran into Rabbi Bernard Raskas at Temple of Aaron in St. Paul and asked for his advice. Though he had only been at that congregation for five years in 1956, he was already one of the leading rabbis in the Twin Cities; he would serve Temple of Aaron for thirty-eight years. He said, "Tom, I would never have chosen this as a fight. But once the Jewish community has made a stand on something like this, we have to follow." That wasn't much solace.

Popovich might not have seen this emblem as a religious symbol when he approved the design. But he saw the criticism as an affront to his faith. Peter was a pretty doctrinaire Catholic. He created another committee, appointed state Sen. Henry Harren from very Catholic Stearns County as its chair, and pledged a meeting on the issue. Meanwhile, some local radio talk shows took off on the issue, and the Unitarians and even the DFL state chairman Ray Hemenway got involved in support of Scheiner's position. But Peter

Minnesota statehood centennial emblem

wasn't inclined to back down. When the commission met in January 1957, it voted 8–2 to keep the controversial symbol.

It was a bad step in our whole procedure, though thankfully the complaints died down before our big year. But the episode hasn't been forgotten. *Minnesota History* magazine published a story about the controversy in 2008, one that erroneously reported that the commission understood from the start that the symbol was a Christian cross. That simply wasn't the case.

THE CENTENNIAL was a yearlong celebration. The highlight was Statehood Week, commencing with a covered wagon trek and Pony Express on Saturday, May 3, and winding up with a rededication ceremony at Memorial Stadium on Sunday, May 11. We pulled out all the stops. Each day had a theme and featured exhibits, luncheons, dinners, dedication ceremonies, concerts—the works. The list of foreign dignitaries who joined us for some or all of that week ran to two full pages in our commemorative program. Twenty-four countries were represented. At the time, we were particularly proud to host Princess Astrid of Norway and Prince Bertil of Sweden, as well as the prime ministers of Norway, Denmark, Iceland, and Finland. In hindsight, the biggest name among the foreign visitors to Minnesota that year was Mohammad Reza Shah Pahlavi, the Shah of Iran, who came in June to look at agricultural practices at the University of Minnesota. He was unmarried at the time, and it seemed as if every Persian mother of a marriageable daughter within one hundred miles of the university tried to get her daughter close to him while he was here. Twenty years later, this same Shah would be deposed at the start of an uprising that led to fifty-two Americans being held hostage for 444 days and, one can argue, to the defeat of President Jimmy Carter by California Governor Ronald Reagan in 1980.

On Saturday, May 10, a three-hour Parade of the Century wound its way from Snelling and Thomas Avenues (just north of University Avenue in St. Paul) to the State Fairgrounds. It was huge—sixty-seven bands, one hundred floats, scores of specialty units. We had fretted for months that it would be cold that day, as it often is in Minnesota in early May. Instead, it was the warmest spring day in memory, with temperatures exceeding 90 degrees! We had high school band kids in heavy woolen uniforms dropping like flies with heat exhaustion. "100 youths collapse as mercury rises," was the headline in the Sunday *Tribune* the next day. Don Padilla gave his old cap to Prince Bertil, who had never experienced hot sunshine like this before.

The parade's grand marshal was Gen. Lauris Norstad, the supreme commander of the Allied Forces in Europe and a native of Minneapolis. He had spent his entire adult life in the military away from Minnesota, but that didn't matter. He was born in Minnesota, and he had done well. That was good enough for us.

The same could be said about our musical headliner at Memorial Stadium the next day—Judy Garland. She had been born Frances Ethel Gumm in Grand Rapids, Minnesota, in 1922. Four years later, her family moved to California, never to return. Nevertheless, we claimed her and persuaded her to sing "God Bless America" and a few other numbers at the grand finale to Statehood Week. Our featured speaker at that event wasn't a Minnesotan but had a governmental rank befitting our many foreign dignitaries—Secretary of State John Foster Dulles. (We'd invited President Eisenhower, but he declined.)

Judy Garland arrived on Friday night. We had a banquet that night to honor General Norstad at the Nicollet Hotel. At the hotel, I found her sitting outside the ballroom, alone and looking a bit lost. I thought that was a bit odd and exchanged a few words with her. News reports later said she came to Minnesota "from her sickbed" and had been suffering laryngitis. I didn't detect that then.

She attended Saturday's big centennial banquet and was photographed singing the national anthem alongside Lt. Gov. Karl Rolvaag. I didn't see her again until Sunday at Memorial Stadium. We had a stage on the field, and behind the stage we'd placed a travel trailer to serve as a dressing room for both Garland and Dulles. I don't remember how, but word came to me that Judy was there and was requesting vodka. It was Sunday. In Minnesota, then and now, liquor stores are closed on Sundays. And even if they had been open, vodka was hard to find in Minnesota. This was the height of the Cold War with the Soviet Union, and vodka was considered a "commie drink." I called Arlene and asked her whether she would drive to Wisconsin and buy some vodka. She told me to go pound sand or something to that effect. I finally found someone willing to make a mad dash to Wisconsin to buy some vodka. Meanwhile, I learned that Judy had locked herself in the trailer and wouldn't come out until performance time. She did, however, open the trailer door when the Wisconsin delivery arrived.

John Foster Dulles was coming into Wold-Chamberlain Field directly from a trip to Europe. His flight was somewhat tardy, and he undoubtedly had that light-headed, disheveled feeling anyone has after a long plane ride across many time zones. Our people rushed him to Memorial Stadium, where it was hot and a big crowd was waiting. Their car pulled up in front of Cooke Hall, situated at one end of the stadium, and Sen. Ed Thye and I went to greet him. The program was underway. He apologized to us for being late. Senator Thye said, "That's all right. We have a spot for you in the trailer where you can quickly freshen up." Dulles brightened a bit at that suggestion.

"No," I interrupted. "We don't have enough time." I knew that if he went to the trailer and it was locked, Dulles's unsuccessful effort to enter would be noticed by all the reporters there. That would be the big story, that Judy Garland locked the secretary of state out of the visitors' trailer.

Dulles graciously went directly to the stage, sat down and looked over the text of his prepared remarks. We'd given him no opportunity to do that in private. Judy's "Selection of Favorites" came shortly before Dulles's speech in the program. He continued to review his notes while she sang and news cameras clicked. The story that Barbara Flanagan of the *Minneapolis Star* wrote for the next day's newspaper said she seemed "jittery." At one point, she stopped, turned to the Minneapolis Symphony conductor and said, "Can I start again? I just missed that lyric. Isn't this terrible? I was trying to be so good."

When she finished her song, she allowed, "This is a great honor, and I'm really just terrified. This place is so damn big." She dabbed her nose at the end of "You Made Me Love You," urged the crowd—and Governor Freeman—to sing along on "For Me and My Gal," and seemed misty-eyed during "Over the Rainbow." At one point, she asked for water and was delivered orange juice instead by U.S. Rep. Walter Judd of Minneapolis. She sipped it, then said, "Boy, it's hot." It wasn't the smoothest performance, and knowing her pre-performance beverage of choice, I thought I knew why. But the crowd loved it.

The next morning, it fell to me to pick her up at the hotel and take her to the airport. To my surprise, she was in tears. Accompanying Flanagan's story in the *Minneapolis Tribune* was a photograph of her belting a song, with an unsmiling John Foster Dulles seated behind her, eyes downcast, going over his speech notes. She was portrayed as being ignored by the secretary of state in a photograph that was likely to be put on the wire and reprinted in newspapers around the world. She was hurt by Dulles's slight and offended that the Minneapolis paper would publish such a thing. I apologized as best I could. It was a surreal coda to an unforgettable weekend.

* * *

WE STAYED IN BUSINESS through 1958 and for a few months in 1959, orchestrating events and eventually settling our accounts. We ended up with $100,000 in unspent funds. That feat was rare enough to warrant prominent mention in a November 23, 1958, feature story in the *New York Times* about Minnesota's banner year. The commission voted to donate the unspent funds to a new public television service being established just then, KTCA-TV. It's today's TPT. It might be said that the station's first studio on Como Avenue, across from the State Fairgrounds, was the final project of the Minnesota Statehood Centennial.

CHAPTER 11

The Wager

P HYSICAL FITNESS WAS ON AMERICANS' MINDS in 1956–57 as President Eisenhower created the first President's Council on Youth Fitness. One of Minnesota's sports heroes, Bud Wilkinson, was involved and would head this program a few years later under President Kennedy. Wilkinson had been the Golden Gophers' star quarterback during Minnesota's national championship years in the 1930s. In the 1950s, he was head football coach at the University of Oklahoma, building its football program into a powerhouse and gaining plenty of fame for himself.

The considerable attention this presidential initiative was getting, and the critique that came with it about the unfit condition of young Americans, made it fodder for dinner party conversations. At one such discussion during a sociable evening hosted by John and Ann Marie Geisler in the fall of 1957, I made a wager with David Speer that made headlines of its own.

Speer was the publicist for the St. Paul Winter Carnival. I had come to know him through my work with the St. Paul Convention and Visitors Bureau. Geisler was his boss at the Carnival. Dave and his father, Ray Speer, had also done some publicity work for the State Fair and for us for the centennial. Arlene first knew him in the late 1930s as an ice-cream customer at McWilliams Drug Store in south Minneapolis. Speer went on to be the public relations business partner of our centennial staff publicist, Don Padilla. David was an outgoing fellow with a ready laugh and a lot of opinions to share.

After a couple of drinks that night, he waxed about how pathetic it was that the people of America were in such bad shape that they needed a presidential call to arms to take better care of themselves. I disagreed. Better nutrition and more sports programs in schools were producing a strong generation, I argued.

Our disagreement led to a wager of $20—a substantial sum for me then—that I could do twice as many push-ups as he could. Down on the floor we went, huffing and puffing through our exertions. It turned out that I could do more than he could—twenty-six, to be exact—but not twice as many. I lost that bet and paid him $20.

I would have left it at that. But David gloried in his victory and kept up his patter about unfit Americans. He challenged me to a sit-up contest, with the same terms as before. I would have to do twice as many as he did to win $20. Again, I outdid him but lost the bet. I did fifty-five sit-ups, compared to his forty-one.

I was out $40 and must have made some comment about how that was not a trivial sum for a guy working for the Centennial Commission. My work on the centennial project was evidently on his mind, given what came out of his mouth next: "I feel so good, I bet I could walk as far as those old pioneers did in a day."

"Could you make it to Mankato in forty-eight hours? Old timers used to do it regularly," I responded—according to the account in the *St. Paul Pioneer Press* column Once Over Lightly, by Paul Light, which was really written by a journalist named Roy Dunlap.

"I believe I could," Dave replied.

"I have $100 that says you can't," I countered.

Dave said he had $100 that said he could. The wager was on. Each of us wrote a check to the other for $100, and we gave the checks for safekeeping and eventual distribution to our flabbergasted host John Geisler. Our agreement was that sometime during Minnesota's centennial year, at a date of Speer's choosing, he would set out to walk to Mankato, eighty-five miles from St. Paul, within forty-eight hours.

Arlene scolded me all the way home that night. No one can walk that far in two days, she said. He was likely to hurt himself trying. What was I thinking?

Dave might have begun to worry about the same thing. A few days later, he mailed me a $20 check, returning a portion of his winnings. I responded by sending the check back to him and informing him that as far as I was concerned, the $100 bet was still on. "If you think for one moment that the possible loss of $20 on the field of battle is going to compromise me into forgetting 'Mankato in forty-eight hours or I lose a C note to Swain,' you're balmy," I wrote in reply. By then, our bet had been described in the *Pioneer Press*. As far as I was concerned, the Walk to Mankato Wager was on.

Speer was too proud to back down. He named his dates, a Saturday and Sunday in late June, I believe. On the stated Saturday, Dave set off from his apartment near Randolph and Snelling in St. Paul. John Geisler's secretary drove ahead of him as support staff, meeting him at rest stops with provisions and an apricot-scented cream for foot massages. After a few hours, Arlene insisted that I take the car and check on him. I cruised Highway 13 without success.

The next day, we called his apartment. Somewhat to our surprise, he answered. I had won the bet, he told me. About midafternoon on Saturday, he decided he would rather have a good dinner at the AAA Auto Club Country Club in Bloomington than press on to Shakopee. He ended his trek and told John Geisler to give me the $100.

A winner of a months-long bet like that is supposed to feel triumphant. But I felt sheepish—maybe because Arlene kept saying what a crazy challenge I'd given Dave. At her insistence, we used the $100 to throw a party for Dave and our mutual friends who knew about the wager. It was a nice occasion that gave him some enjoyment in return for sore feet and a bruised ego.

CHAPTER 12

Showboat

I̲T̲ ̲W̲A̲S̲ ̲I̲N̲E̲V̲I̲T̲A̲B̲L̲E̲ ̲I̲N̲ ̲T̲H̲E̲ 1950s: any civic celebration had to have a beauty queen. The women's movement that would call such notions into question was still more than a decade away. The Centennial Commission decided early on that we needed a Miss Centennial Minnesota.

That's how I found myself in Austin, Minnesota, as a judge of the 1956 Miss Minnesota pageant. I was there to build connections that would benefit the centennial observance soon after. The 1957 pageant winner would carry the title "Miss Centennial Minnesota" and have special responsibilities for appearances at centennial events in 1958, both in Minnesota and around the country. We would be sending delegations to other state or city festivals, and often Miss Centennial Minnesota would be part of the troupe.

The 1957 winner was Diane Albers of Dundas, a student at St. Olaf College and a very winsome young woman. We kept her so busy that year that we decided she needed housing in St. Paul. I arranged for her to live with our widowed next-door neighbor, Esther Arouni. I also found an older couple to be her chaperones and de facto bodyguards. Years before, these people had lived in southern California and had supplied much the same service to up-and-coming movie actress Joan Crawford. They were full of Hollywood stories to keep Diane entertained.

Judging the 1956 pageant brought me into contact with another judge, Frank Whiting, the much-respected director of the University of Minnesota theater program. What a great human being he was! We struck up a conversation while sitting together in the grandstand during a parade in connection with the pageant. He confided that his lifelong ambition was to establish a showboat that would be moored near campus in the Mississippi River and used for summer theatrical productions.

Whiting didn't want just a unique setting. He wanted to preserve the kind of entertainment that showboats brought to river towns in the late nineteenth and early twentieth centuries. They would present plays, often melodramas, into which song-and-dance musical numbers had been inserted to add humor and interest. Those song-and-dance features, called olios, were vaudeville-style entertainment that audiences loved and that Whiting was keen to preserve.

I thought, I'm heading an organization that's getting a train on loan from the Great Northern railroad, decking it out with historic artifacts, and sending it on a 135-day tour of the state. A centennial showboat? That can't be too hard, can it? I came back from the pageant and told Don Padilla, "Let's start scouting around for an old riverboat." We found a fellow in Ohio named Freeman who specialized in this sort of thing. After a few false leads—one too small, one too large, one too expensive—we learned that a packet boat, the *General John Newton,* based in New Orleans, was being declared surplus. Built in 1899, it spanned 175 feet and had a picturesque paddlewheel. It had been a U.S. Army Corps of Engineers "hearing boat" on the lower Mississippi, the scene of official government meetings. Three U.S. presidents had been aboard.

Best of all, the price was right. We could have it for $1, provided we used it for educational purposes. Of course, we'd have to pay for its renovation. Naively, we didn't think that would be too daunting. U.S. Sen. Ed Thye of Minnesota helped us deal with the Army Corps of Engineers to claim the *General John Newton.* When the two U.S. senators from Louisiana heard about our transaction, they were unhappy and tried to stop it. But Thye made sure the deal stuck—though Hubert Humphrey usually got the credit. The *Minneapolis Star* and *Tribune* paid for bringing it up the river from New Orleans to Minnesota.

Frank Whiting was thrilled. However, his department had only $25,000 to contribute to transforming the *Newton* into the Centennial Showboat. That sum represented his entire theater department reserves. We contributed $25,000 in centennial funds. But that wasn't enough. For this boat to sail, some additional donations would be needed.

To the rescue came James Lewis Morrill. By 1957, he had been president of the university for twelve years. In all that time, he had avoided personally soliciting donations from would-be benefactors—something that's hard to imagine any collegiate president escaping today. But soon after we learned that the showboat project was short of funds, President Morrill and I were making calls on 3M and some other major firms. He'd even pick me up at my office for these errands. He told me I was witnessing what was for him a first.

"Why are you doing this, Dr. Morrill?" I asked him.

"I just love that Frank Whiting," he replied.

Morrill proved very effective. We were able to get the showboat in shape for quite a tour in the summer of 1958. It was never self-ambulatory, but it was towed—or tugged—to St. Paul, Stillwater, Hastings, Red Wing, Wabasha, and Winona for performances. Frank Whiting and his wife lived in the captain's wheelhouse during part of that summer. That's how much he loved that boat. The student performers that first summer would say fifty years later that being in the inaugural showboat cast was the highlight of their college days.

THAT KIND OF TOURING was eventually deemed too expensive, and the ship stayed moored at its home base on Washington Flats, down the river bluff from the Minneapolis campus. By 1993, it had badly deteriorated and was closed for renovation. Sadly, a few years later, a welder's torch went awry and the old *General John Newton* burned to the hull. But Minnesota theater audiences weren't going to let go of Whiting's dream. Funds were raised, a partnership was established between the university and the Padelford Riverboat Co., a new boat was built, and in 2002 it was permanently docked at Harriet Island near downtown St. Paul. Fittingly, the new boat is named the *Frank M. Whiting.*

The new boat arrived with its interior largely unfinished. It was a replay of 1957–58. We had to scramble again to raise money to complete the project. At one point, I was told that sufficient funds had been secured to provide the theater but not to finish its balcony. That won't do, I said. A showboat is not a showboat without a balcony. We kept raising money until we could afford a balcony too. That's why, if you visit the University of Minnesota Centennial Showboat today, you will see a little plaque naming the balcony for me.

CHAPTER 13

Skål, Vikings—and Stay, Twins

As THE CENTENNIAL CELEBRATION WOUND DOWN, I had several tempting job offers. Arlene and I decided that with children heading toward college in a few years, my next job should be in the private sector, with stable income and opportunity for growth. But I had loved the centennial project and relished the idea of starting something new. That's why I agreed to become the first executive director of the Minnesota Insurance Information Center, a new industry-established consumer education project to which nearly every insurance company domiciled in the state contributed. It was another chance to build something from scratch.

I was busy setting up the Insurance Information Center's headquarters in the venerable Soo Line Building in Minneapolis. Built in 1915, it had been the Soo Line Railroad's headquarters, and for fourteen years it had the distinction of being the tallest building in Minnesota: nineteen stories. Our office meant to better inform Minnesotans about property and casualty insurance and to tamp down discontent over high auto insurance premiums, which were a growing concern in Minnesota. We created a filmstrip, *Auto Insurance and You*, that I used in speaking engagements with high school students. State law required drivers to be insured. By the late 1950s, the streetcars had disappeared, and cars were king among teenagers. The expense of auto insurance was an impediment to driving for some and an annoyance to many more. When I went to high schools to speak, I was facing a tough audience. But volunteer work I did in the fall of 1959 put me before what may have been my toughest audience ever.

Working in downtown Minneapolis gave me proximity to a sports booster group called the Minnesota Minute Men, whose purpose was to bring professional football to the Twin Cities. In

1959 the Minute Men had their eyes on the Chicago Cardinals, a team that was financially foundering in Chicago's Comiskey Park as the city's number-two NFL franchise. Its owner, widow Violet Bidwill, was looking to move the team to a more lucrative venue. (In 1960, the team would move to St. Louis; today, after another move in 1988, they are the Arizona Cardinals.) The Minute Men contracted with the Cardinals to play two 1959 regular-season games at three-year-old Metropolitan Stadium in Bloomington. It was a stadium built on spec, one might say. It had been home to the minor league Minneapolis Millers baseball team since 1956. Its developers had bigger ideas. They intended to lure major league football and baseball franchises.

The Season of Two Games that the Minute Men conceived was a trial run. The goal was to convince Mrs. Bidwill and the NFL to move the Cardinals to Minnesota—or failing that, to locate another franchise at Met Stadium as soon as possible. That meant the stakes were high for the Minnesota hosts of the two Chicago Cardinals games, October 25 against the Philadelphia Eagles and November 22 against the New York Giants. The Minute Men had to fill the stands, and the stadium had to perform to major league standards.

I functioned as the events' business manager and hired a local ticket manager for the two games. Attracting a major league team was too important to the national reputation and future growth potential of the Twin Cities for us to skimp on ticket staffing. Leigh Morawetz of the Downtown Ticket Office agreed to be our ticket man for the bargain rate of $700 per game.

We were keen to fill the stands, so we priced the tickets accordingly. A "season ticket" to both games, the same seat for each, went for $10. A single-game ticket cost $6 for most seats, but only $4 for bleacher seats behind the southern goalposts. The Gophers were playing Michigan and Wisconsin, respectively, at Memorial Stadium those same weekends, so we promoted the idea that football fans could see two top-notch games on the same weekend. We promised that "ticket buyers for the two 1959 games will have priority on all professional games played here in the future." We weren't sure what we were promising, but we liked the optimism of that line.

We guaranteed the Cardinals $240,000 to play in Blooming-ton and expected to raise that sum without difficulty. But to be on the safe side, the Minute Men went to business owners, mostly modest-sized local firms, and got guarantees that if an insufficient number of tickets were sold, the businesses would make up for any shortfall. The pitch was that these guarantees were hardly necessary. Our tickets were so inexpensive and the attraction so appealing that the games would be sellouts.

Our prediction held up fairly well for the October 25 game between the Cardinals and the Philadelphia Eagles, whose quar-terback was someone Minnesota football fans would come to know well, future Vikings coach Norm Van Brocklin. But it soon became clear that we were falling considerably short for the second game, the Cards versus the Giants. Sales were just not there for a game in late November in an open-air stadium between two teams with no connection to Minnesota. The guarantors were going to be hit.

About ten days before that game, our Professional Football Executive Committee met to discuss the situation. (Headed by Gerald Moore of the Downtown Council, this committee natu-rally included Charlie Johnson and Sid Hartman of the *Star* and *Tribune*. It was a different era in sports journalism.) I proposed that we call the guarantors together to inform them that our suppos-edly secure bet had turned sour. Further, I suggested, we should give each of them several hundred tickets that they could give to employees, friends, customers, or charities. That way, the guaran-tors could get some benefit, and we could fill the place up and make it look suitably "major league."

"We can't do that!" Gerry Moore said. "These guys will just fly apart on us, they'll be so mad!"

"Maybe so," I countered. "But this is better than doing nothing and sending them a bill afterward."

The group thought it over and came around to my way of think-ing. "But you're going to be the one to make the presentation," Moore told me.

That's how I wound up at the North American Life and Casu-alty Co. headquarters at Hennepin and Groveland Avenues in Min-neapolis, standing before a hastily summoned meeting of local business guarantors to discuss the problem we were having with the second game. North American's chief executive was H. P. Skoglund, an active Minute Man who would become one of the five original owners of the Minnesota Vikings. He was on hand, but I did the talking. I broke the news. Moore and the others were so right. This group exploded in anger at how they'd been misled.

Finally somebody said, "Let's calm down. It's going to cost us, but at least they're offering us something—tickets." With that, the grumbling subsided enough for us to distribute the tickets.

The guarantors put those tickets to good use. On November 22, Met Stadium was full of cheering fans, some of whom had paid nothing to attend and accordingly were willing to spend more freely on concessions. Those proceeds stayed in Minnesota, bringing needed revenue to the Metropolitan Sports Area Commission.

The NFL was duly impressed. The Chicago Cardinals headed for St. Louis, not Minnesota, but at the NFL owners' meeting in January 1960, the comment was made, "If people in Minnesota will come to a game in late November between two teams that are not their own, it must mean that they're ready for professional football." Minnesota got its Vikings.

THE WASHINGTON SENATORS baseball team became the Minnesota Twins the same year the Vikings arrived, 1961. I cheered along with the rest of the state as the Twins came close to winning a World Series in 1965, then succeeded in 1987 and 1991 in a fashion that seemed to bring the whole state together. That unifying spirit proved the worth of major league sports in an increasingly diverse, disparate metropolitan area.

That sense of the Twins' value inspired me to accept an invitation to join Minnesotans for Major League Baseball in 2000. It was a 130-member group assembled by the Twins in hopes of selling politicians and the public on a new ballpark. Without their own facility and sole control over the revenue stream it would generate, the team-owning Pohlad family said, they'd be obliged to either sell or move the team to a more financially congenial environment. The Twins had endured sharing the Metrodome with the Vikings since 1982. It was poorly suited for baseball, even though it was the team's home field when it won two World Series. As the team struggled on the field, and the Metrodome, which had been built on the cheap, rapidly showed its age, attendance at Twins games plummeted in the 1990s. Something had to be done if Minnesota was going to stay on the MLB (Major League Baseball) map.

Minnesotans for Major League Baseball was headed by Karla Blomberg, now president of Wishes & More, and Tom Reagan, a former aide to U.S. Rep. Jim Oberstar and former chair of the University of Minnesota Board of Regents. Though instigated by the Twins, the group provided an independent look at the team's situation by people of such stature and community connections that they could not be accused of rubber-stamping the team's desires. After a number of months of study, the group recommended construction of a baseball-only stadium for the Twins, to be financed half by the team and half via a public financing mechanism involving taxes on tickets and items sold at the ballpark. General tax revenues were not to be used.

I became very involved, as did former DFL Attorney General Warren Spannaus. We became a sales team, testifying together at the Legislature to explain our committee's thinking. After a House committee refused to send the ballpark bill to the full House, Warren and I wrote a commentary essay published in the *Star Tribune*. "We started out as new-stadium skeptics," we wrote. "Why was the 19-year-old Metrodome already obsolete? . . . We're now convinced that without a new park the Twins cannot generate the local revenue to consistently field a competitive team." In the Metrodome, the number of seats with sight lines adequate to command top-dollar ticket prices was small. Concession and parking revenues were shared with the Vikings. Suites were few in number and low in quality. "A new facility is sorely needed," we concluded.

The *Star Tribune* essay got wide notice. Speaking invitations began to arrive. I went to Milwaukee with Spannaus and Twins president Jerry Bell for a private discussion with MLB commissioner Bud Selig to help him better understand Minnesota's thinking.

It seemed that public opinion might be turning in favor of a new home for the Twins. But success at the Legislature was still five years, one state financial crisis, and one big threat of MLB contraction away. Spannaus and I predicted the contraction threat in our 2001 essay. We said that the league would soon realize that "it makes sense to take out a loan, buy up the Twins franchise, put it on the shelf, and save the projected approximately $50 million annual subsidy" that the league would soon have to provide to keep the Twins in business in the Metrodome. That indeed was the league's thinking by the winter of 2002–3. Fortunately, a federal judge put the brakes on the league's contraction idea. In 2003 the Twins started winning again, attendance and the economy improved, and in 2006 the Legislature gave the green light for construction of Target Field.

At one point during those years of stadium discussions, the Twins' general counsel took me aside and said, "You'd make a damned good lawyer." I think he meant it as a compliment.

CHAPTER 14

Elmer for Governor

A MONG THE JOB OFFERS I TURNED DOWN when I agreed to be executive director of the Minnesota Insurance Information Center was a tempting one from former state Sen. Elmer L. Andersen. His offer: come to work as my special assistant at H. B. Fuller Co. and help prepare a campaign for governor in 1960.

I'd worked with Andersen enough on the centennial statue committee to think highly of him. Elmer was twelve years my senior. He'd been owner and president of H. B. Fuller, a St. Paul–based industrial adhesives company, since 1941, building it from a tiny one-factory operation on Eagle Street, near the Mississippi River, into a multinational company. Elmer had done well in business, but he came from humble beginnings. The third child of a Norwegian immigrant and his Scandinavian American wife, Elmer was born in Chicago. His parents' marriage failed when he was about five, and thereafter he was raised by his mother and some doting aunts in Muskegon, Michigan. He came to Minnesota as a young man, met and married Eleanor Johnson, graduated with a business degree from the University of Minnesota, and proceeded to mix business with his many other interests, including public service.

Elmer retired from the state Senate in 1958 after ten years in office, but he wasn't done with politics. He had his eye on running against DFL Gov. Orville Freeman in 1960. He said later in life that when he decided not to run for another term in the Senate, he had no intention to run for governor. That may indeed describe his thinking at the end of his last full legislative session in 1957, but by the end of 1958, the idea of running for governor was firmly in his mind. Though he might have welcomed any thoughts I would have about making and selling industrial adhesives, my real assignment at H. B. Fuller would be to lay the groundwork for a bid for governor. He said he admired the organizational skill I'd exhibited on the centennial project and allowed that a statewide political campaign would have some of the same components—county committees, volunteers, special events, parades and festivals, and plenty of publicity.

He was right about that. But I turned him down because I doubted that my next job should be in politics. "I like politics on the fringes, but I don't have much taste for it on the inside," said my letter declining his offer in January 1959. I added my sincere encouragement and support for his intentions for 1960. "Your ability, integrity and honor are qualities that the state of Minnesota needs and, I trust, will avail themselves of in 1960."

"Ability, integrity and honor." That was my assessment of Elmer Andersen after knowing him only briefly and superficially. After coming to know him much better over the next forty-five years, I would use the same words today, only more emphatically. He had rare leadership ability, grounded in innate respect for others, and enthusiasm for any effort to improve life in Minnesota. He also had a level of integrity and honor unsurpassed by anyone I have known in public life.

We saw in each other similar attitudes and approaches to life. In his 2000 autobiography, *A Man's Reach,* Elmer counted me among a few key friends whose encouragement to run for governor mattered most to him. He described our connection this way: "It is in both of our natures to take life seriously. Life is not an entertainment vehicle. Life is an accomplishment vehicle. Real living is working, doing something and making a difference. It is hard for Tom, as it is hard for me, to stand by when a problem presents itself. We want to pitch in and do something about it. I trusted Tom, he believed in me, and so our lives were linked."

In 1959, we weren't linked yet. I was busy establishing a new venture for the local insurance industry. But I also believed that to make democracy work, good people have to help good people obtain elective office. I volunteered to serve on Elmer's endorsement campaign committee and was on hand when he made his candidacy official on January 5, 1960. I helped him connect with others in a position to be helpful. Elmer credited me with introducing him to Otto Silha, the vice president and chief operating officer of the *Star* and *Tribune* and a major donor to Republican candidates.

Perhaps the most important connection I helped him make was to Don Padilla, our centennial publicity genius. He became Elmer's campaign publicist, which was a big job in the lean campaign Elmer intended to run. Elmer didn't believe in loaning his campaign large sums, and—as was typical in those more genteel days—he left the fund-raising to his finance committee. His instructions to them: don't go into debt. The budget for the whole campaign was only $175,000. (Today, some legislative campaigns spend more than that.) That was a challenge for our very able treasurer, David Lilly, the CEO of Toro Co. We were lucky to have him. Our nickname for him—Skinflint Lilly—was affectionate but deserved.

Campaign staffing was at a minimum. Don was a combination speechwriter / brochure designer / advance man and traveling companion. He helped Elmer write and place a column every two weeks in the state's daily newspapers, explaining his positions. I don't believe we bought any TV ads that year; Elmer's may have been the last major-party gubernatorial campaign in Minnesota not to.

But Don wasn't Elmer's driver. Candidates today are well advised to hire a driver and use him or her consistently. Don't risk getting behind the wheel yourself. That advice evidently wasn't heard much in 1960—or if Elmer heard it, he disregarded it. He'd started in business as a traveling salesman. He liked to drive. He had a Ford—not a fancy car, but one big enough to chauffeur others and serve as a mobile meeting room. Being a good salesman, he was trained to make eye contact when engaged in a sales conversation—a habit that worried his campaign committee because his passengers were often in the back seat. Later in the campaign, we converted a pickup truck into a campaign-mobile, complete with a little office in the back end.

Elmer's focus all spring was on a contest for Republican endorsement with the mayor of Minneapolis, P. Kenneth Peterson. P. Kenneth was a good guy from a big family and a former legislator. His brother C. Donald Peterson was in the Legislature in 1960 and eventually had a distinguished career on the Minnesota Supreme Court. Kenneth's wife Jean Ann and I were friends; she had been a secretary to Republican Gov. Luther Youngdahl. But I was working hard for Elmer that year, and their contest stirred up strong feelings within a party that was already dividing between liberal thinkers and more conservative ones, including Peterson. Then and for the rest of his life, Elmer proudly called himself a liberal Republican, much in favor of civil rights, public education, and a helping hand to the poor.

Just how intense the contest was that spring became obvious at the Second District Republican convention in New Ulm, where delegates to the state convention would be chosen. I was standing in the corridor chatting with another Elmer supporter, Kay Harmon. She was chairwoman of the Second District and was a vivacious, outgoing person who told others what she thought.

Some guy who was a Kenny Peterson supporter came by. He made some strong remarks; Kay replied in kind; his language turned crude in response. I came to Kay's defense. The next thing I knew, he and I were wrestling in the corridor. I felt a little sheepish when others gathered around to break up the tussle. "I was supporting Kay Harmon," I explained. "I wasn't going to let anybody talk to her like that." It was the last time I let something like that happen.

After that excitement, the state Republican convention was an anticlimax. Peterson was persuaded at the last minute to drop out of the governor's race and run against U.S. Sen. Hubert Humphrey, who was seeking his third term and had become a national leader in the Democratic Party. Given Humphrey's popularity, Peterson was making a sacrificial move.

Not long after the state convention, Elmer called. A strong convention sendoff and a united party fueled his confidence. If he ran a smart campaign all summer and fall against Freeman, he said, he could win, despite the appeal of the rest of the Democratic Party's ticket that presidential year. But he needed a campaign manager. Would I reconsider my decision of eighteen months earlier and come to work for him?

Elmer's question presented me with one of the toughest and biggest choices of my life. All the reasons that I cited in 1959 to stay in the private sector were just as valid in 1960. But working as a volunteer on Elmer's campaign committee had been more rewarding than I expected—and if the campaign succeeded, the result would be more important for Minnesota than helping consumers better understand property and casualty insurance. Arlene was an Elmer fan too, which helped me decide. You've got to put yourself where your mouth is. I helped select a new president for the Insurance Information Center—Bob Provost, who would hold that position for more than thirty years and become something of a household name through a weekly WCCO radio program. Then I reported for work at the Andersen for Governor campaign headquarters in an abandoned savings-and-loan office in downtown St. Paul.

Elmer was a businessman with a businesslike approach to campaigning. He knew what he wanted to do and say and didn't need a lot of advice about that. As for the rest—fund-raising, advertising, volunteer recruitment, logistics—he believed in delegating authority to others. That gave me considerable latitude. I had never run a political campaign before, but Elmer was right: it was a lot like organizing the centennial.

I don't think Elmer and I ever had an argument, during that campaign or at any other time. We disagreed from time to time, but with him, disagreements weren't arguments. They were respectful conversations. He said he appreciated my willingness to tell him when I had an opinion or idea that differed from his.

We decided to make the Eighth District in northeastern Minnesota a special target of the campaign. That wasn't typical Republican strategy. In those years the Eighth District typically voted for DFLers over Republicans by what seemed like an eight-to-one majority. We figured if we could cut that majority even to four-to-one, we could swing 20,000 votes our way. The economy was soft there. We could campaign on the premise that Orville Freeman hasn't delivered for this part of the state, and it's time for a change.

Part of my involvement in the Eighth District was to recruit a committee of mayors—Mayors for Elmer Andersen. These were great guys—Joe Jagunich of Eveleth, Joe Taveggia of Hibbing, Doc Grahek of Ely, Benny Constantine, a former Eveleth mayor, and a few others. I had a lot of fun with them. They felt they were being taken for granted by the DFL, and things needed to change. But they were also wary of being too visible in their support of a

Republican. They were something of a secret society that summer and fall, advising us behind the scenes.

Elmer was eager to visit that part of the state. (In fact, he was always willing to get out and meet people—even when he was sick and running a fever. He was indefatigable.) Elmer had real respect and affection for the hardworking people of northeastern Minnesota. Many of them were the children of immigrants, as he was himself. They reminded him of the people he knew in Muskegon. Elmer would walk down the street in the towns on the Range or in Duluth hoping to shake a few hands. Some people would ignore his outstretched hand and pass pretty quickly. They wouldn't dare be seen shaking hands with a Republican. But then they'd mutter as they went by, "I'm with ya! Good luck!"

SOMEHOW WE WON OVER JENO PAULUCCI, a great Minnesota entrepreneur and one of the most voluble characters in Duluth. In those years, Paulucci's chief business venture was the Chun King line of canned Chinese food, which he founded in the 1940s and sold in 1966. He went on to build, then sell, a number of other food product lines, including his most famous food innovation, the pizza roll. Jeno was a native of Aurora, a mining town on the Iron Range, and he still cared a great deal about Iron Range affairs. He had a great distrust for the Oliver Iron Mining Co., a major employer in his hometown. He told me he was willing to help Elmer in exchange for one favor, should Elmer win. He wanted a hand in the appointment of the Andersen administration's commissioner of the Iron Range Resources and Rehabilitation Board, that region's tax-funded economic redevelopment organization. I thought that was a reasonable request and persuaded Elmer to agree to it. It turned out that Jeno wanted a whale of a lot more, but that came later.

I got along famously with Jeno. Not everybody did. At one point during the campaign, the *Duluth Herald Tribune* misquoted a leader in the mining industry saying something about assurances the industry had from Elmer. Jeno's habit was to pick up his mail and his daily newspaper at the Duluth post office very early every morning, including Saturdays and Sundays, and go through it right away. The article with the error was published on a Sunday. Jeno was still at the post office when he read it. He exploded in anger. The word was that the postal workers were ducking behind the counter to steer clear of him. Then he called me. It was about five or six in the morning. I didn't know what had happened but told him I'd find out. It took me the rest of the day to track it down and determine that the newspaper had simply dropped a negation, changing the meaning of the quote. The paper would correct the error, I told Jeno. But by then, the episode had so distressed Jeno that he went into seclusion for a week. He wasn't available for anything. He thought that somehow he had been double-crossed.

Jeno finally got over that and was full of ideas for northeastern Minnesota after Elmer was elected. I advised him to enlist public support for some of his ideas. They weren't things one person could do solo. He took that advice sufficiently to heart to form NEMO, the Northeast Minnesota Organization. He even hired an executive director, Lee Vann, who had been head of the Minnesota Arrowhead Association, a tourism promotion group. However, we soon saw that Jeno was incapable of getting people together and getting them to think collaboratively. It was his way or the highway.

At one point in 1961 he became exceedingly impatient with the Legislature. He wanted action on a constitutional amendment that would assure taconite companies that their property would be taxed on the same basis and rate as any other manufacturing plant would be. Elmer backed that amendment, but it was met with skepticism or worse among legislators, including many from the Iron Range. Meanwhile, a bill to make the loon the state bird of Minnesota was consuming an inordinate amount of time and attention. This distressed Jeno greatly. His response was to buy thirty minutes of prime time on a Twin Cities television station. He planned to spend the full half hour addressing a stuffed loon perched before him on a table. I thought it was a terrible idea. It would make laughingstocks of both him and the taconite amendment, I predicted. But if anyone could pull it off, Jeno Paulucci could. To my surprise, it came off remarkably well.

There was an issue involving freight rates for shipping goods by rail or boat to Chicago. Jeno was sure the railroads were overcharging. Elmer asked me to call a meeting of some railroad executives and Paulucci, to see if we could be instrumental in obtaining more equitable shipping rates for northeastern Minnesota. We persuaded John Budd, the president of the Great Northern, and Robert Macfarlane, the head of the Northern Pacific, and a few other CEOs to come to a meeting at the Minnesota Club and hear Jeno out. Jeno arrived early, so I took him aside. "Jeno, you've got to promise me one thing. Don't lose your temper. You just can't do that with this group. They've come as a favor to Governor Andersen."

I was presiding over the meeting. When everyone was introduced, I called on Jeno to explain his concern. He got about five sentences into his story when he took off. He started berating those railroad executives. As a result, this wasn't a productive meeting. Afterward, I said, "Jeno, for God's sake! Why did you do that?"

"I can't help it, Tom," he said. "I get so angry."

It was inevitable that eventually Jeno would become unhappy with Elmer. In 1962, he supported Elmer's challenger, DFLer Karl Rolvaag. I'll get ahead of my story to report here that Elmer would lose that election in what is still the closest gubernatorial contest in U.S. history. Thirty-eight years later, Jeno wrote Elmer a characteristically modest letter claiming that his desertion had single-handedly caused Elmer's loss. Then he added, "I don't know if it was the right thing to do because you are a person that I always admired. . . . I'm proud to have known you, proud to have been your friend, proud to have been your adversary and always a person who respected you for what you really are, a great man."

NEAR THE END OF THE 1960 CAMPAIGN, we invited New York Gov. Nelson Rockefeller to appear with Elmer in northeastern Minnesota. Elmer had become acquainted with Rockefeller along the way, and they'd hit it off. We decided to bring him to the Eighth District because the Rockefeller name was well regarded there. Nelson's grandfather John D. Rockefeller had been a major investor in the Mesabi Range and in the railroad and shipping businesses that moved Minnesota ore to foundries in places like Cleveland, Pittsburgh, and Buffalo.

Nelson joined Elmer for a day that started at Hibbing High School, the most palatial high school building in the state and perhaps in the country. That's because Oliver Iron Mining Co. required the entire town of Hibbing to move two miles south in 1920–21 and tried to soothe unhappy residents by providing $4 million, a huge sum in those days, for the construction of a new high school. A big crowd filled the 1,800-seat auditorium, where Rockefeller marveled at the chandeliers from Belgium. That event was a success. Then we had a caravan across the Range. Nelson was a handsome fellow with a reputation as a ladies' man. I remember female nurses in uniform lining the parade route to get a glimpse of him and Nelson insisting on stopping to shake hands.

We were to finish at a vacant theater on Duluth's north side and then had to get him to the airport on time to fly to the Twin Cities, where he would make a campaign appearance with Third District Republican congressional candidate Clark MacGregor. The Mac-Gregor people were somewhat suspicious of us. It was up to me to stay on schedule and see to it that Nelson Rockefeller made the trip as planned.

As luck would have it, we were running late. I was concerned. We got to the Duluth theater and found a large crowd waiting both inside and outside. We were scheduled to stop at the front where the crowd was assembled and let out the principals. But I said no. "We're short on time. Let's go to the back and get them into the theater right away."

When we got inside, Rockefeller approached me and asked, "Who was responsible for dropping us off in the back?"

"I am," I said.

"Don't ever do that again! If people are here to see me, I want to be seen," he said. He gave me a real chewing out. I tried to mumble something about Clark MacGregor but couldn't get it out. I kept thinking, "Here I am, being chewed out by one of the most famous men in America."

Sure enough, he was late in arriving at the MacGregor event, and the MacGregor people blamed me. But the Rockefeller–Andersen friendship was sealed for the rest of their lives.

OUR EIGHTH DISTRICT STRATEGY PAID OFF. Freeman still carried the district, but we cut his share of the vote in the district's dominant St. Louis County from 70 percent to 59 percent and gained nearly 18,000 votes over the 1958 Republican candidate for governor, George MacKinnon. Better still, we won the election by nearly 23,000 votes. Elmer was on his way to the governor's office—and I was going along.

CHAPTER 15

Right Hand to the Governor

WHEN ELMER ASKED ME to be chief of staff in the governor's office—officially "executive secretary" in those years—I didn't hesitate to say yes. By that point, I was all in. If you support somebody for elective office and that person asks you to do something to advance his mission, you ought to do it. Elmer made the decision easier by seeing to it that I would not make a financial sacrifice to work for him. His own salary as governor in 1961 was only $19,000.

My job was to bring more efficiency to the governor's office. One of Elmer's campaign promises had been to cut the cost of state operations. He'd been explicit about the governor's office budget. He wanted it cut in half. Elmer Andersen never said anything lightly when it came to state government. He meant it, and we had to do it. I was lucky to have the assistance of Joanne Juers, a Carleton College grad who had helped us on the centennial staff. She became my secretary.

Our task was made particularly difficult by the deluge of applications for jobs and appointments we received from Republican activists. The Republican Party had been out of the governor's office for six years, after dominating state politics for most of the first one hundred years of statehood. A lot of people who were used to state employment wanted jobs. Elmer's fiscal decree meant that there would be fewer patronage positions to fill. Years later in his autobiography, Elmer said, "One might fairly conclude that right from the start, I was working pretty hard on losing votes in the next election."

One of the things we concluded is that we needed to eliminate some of the regulatory and advisory boards that tend to proliferate in state government. On our list for elimination, with Elmer's blessing, was the Board of Watchmaking. When individual craftsmen made watches, it made sense that a board would set standards and certify that a watch's design met them. In the modern era of mass production, it no longer did—or so I thought. It turned out that the board employed a lawyer at a considerable sum, and that lawyer had a friend in Republican state Sen. Robert Dunlap, a Wabasha County prosecutor whose father and brother had both been managing editors of the *St. Paul Pioneer Press* and *Dispatch*. Dunlap was a decent man, the chair of the powerful Senate Education Committee, and an old-fashioned conservative. He didn't cotton to a lot of change, and he was loyal to his friends. "What are you rocking the boat for?" he asked me about our plan for the Board of Watchmaking. "Leave these folks alone. They're not hurting anybody." I went back to Elmer and asked, "Is it worth alienating Bob Dunlap to get rid of this thing?" It stayed.

Elmer was more determined when it came to closing some of the little highway equipment garages that dotted the landscape in rural Minnesota. He stuck to his guns despite an outcry in some places with garages, including the little town of Fertile near the North Dakota border. That town had backed him by a three-to-one margin in 1960. It went three-to-one against him in 1962. Elmer used to say, "There's only so much good government that people can stand."

The mandate to cut the number of positions in the governor's office meant that the staff and I were working long hours. We were a hardworking, dedicated bunch, but it was tough. At one point, I appealed for help to some of the Liberal Caucus legislators who controlled the state House. (This was before party designation came to the Legislature and the Liberal Caucus took the Democratic-Farmer-Labor Party label.) At that time, we were getting along better with the Liberals than with the Conservatives who controlled the Senate, even though Elmer had been a Conservative senator for ten years. "We're having a tough time getting all the work done," I told those legislators. Would they quietly supplement the appropriation we were seeking for the governor's office?

They may have agreed with us on some policy questions, but those legislators were partisan politicians and we were their Republican adversaries. "We'll consider it if you publicly ask for it," they said. There was no way I could do that, not after Elmer campaigned on trimming the cost of government. We soldiered on.

ELMER HAD ALWAYS BEEN MORE LIBERAL than many of the members of his old Senate caucus. For example, Elmer disagreed with the Conservatives' push to substitute a sales tax, which Minnesota did not yet have, for a portion of the state's income tax. A sales tax is regressive, Elmer argued. It falls disproportionately on lower- and middle-income people. Elmer didn't think that was fair or economically sound policy. (As a result, Minnesota wouldn't institute a sales tax until four years after Elmer left office.)

That difference of opinion led to some strained relationships. I saw a little of that for myself the night after he decided to appoint James Otis to the state Supreme Court. Otis came from a long line of distinguished St. Paul attorneys and had been a lower-court judge for thirteen years. He was more than qualified. But he was a pro–civil rights liberal from the big city. Elmer and I went to dinner at the Minnesota Club the night he made his choice, and there was state Sen. Gordon Rosenmeier, the Conservative lion of the Senate. Elmer seldom saw eye-to-eye with Rosenmeier, but he had great respect for him. He decided to go to Rosenmeier's table and personally deliver the news about Otis's appointment. I watched Rosenmeier's face and saw him half-exploding. Rosenmeier, from Little Falls, had favored the appointment of someone more conservative from his part of the state. Elmer had to know that reaction was coming. But doing what was right for the state mattered more to him than currying favor with legislators, even the great Gordon Rosenmeier.

Otis provided acclaimed service on the Supreme Court and moral leadership in the community. He took a stand against racial discrimination in the Exchange Club of St. Paul, where I was a member, that led to that chapter agreeing to leave its national organization and change its name to The St. Paul Club. That departure required the resignation of every club member, lest a remnant be able to retain all the club's assets. Otis secured every member's signature.

All three of Elmer's Supreme Court appointees were stellar. The others were Walter Rogosheske and Robert Sheran, both great human beings. (I'll say more about the Sheran appoinment later.) Elmer was careful and deliberate in his judicial appointments, and he sometimes used me as a sounding board. He said that appointments to the bench were a governor's most enduring legacy.

He was just as careful about state agency appointments and just as unwilling to let party affiliation guide his decisions. If a Democrat was the best qualified for the job or was already in office and performing well, Elmer didn't hesitate to appoint him, to the consternation of Republican activists. One such case involved the reappointment of the chair of the commission on municipal annexation, Joe Robbie, an attorney and native South Dakotan. Only a few years later, when the Miami Dolphins football team was created, Joe became one of its owners, thanks in part to his relationship with then NFL commissioner and former South Dakota Gov. Joe Foss. He would go on to be the team's sole owner. For a time, the Dolphins' stadium was named Joe Robbie Stadium. But in 1961, Robbie wasn't yet known for football. Minnesota Republicans knew him as a Democrat who had once run unsuccessfully for governor of South Dakota.

That didn't matter to Elmer. When Robbie's term on the municipal annexation commission was about to expire, he asked me to check him out. I learned that he had been doing a fine job, so Elmer reappointed him. Republicans went nuts in response. We had angry calls and letters: "Don't you understand party loyalty?" Elmer did, but he didn't think it ought to trump all other considerations.

ELMER BELIEVED IN ACCOUNTABILITY and accessibility to the people. He announced that he would be available in his office one night per week to meet with citizens who wanted to voice their concerns, and that twice per week he would make himself available to journalists at a news conference. These were well-intentioned ideas that at times proved difficult to execute. A colorful group of citizens took to coming to his Capitol "office hours," but they accomplished little. Twice weekly news conferences taxed our capacity to supply Capitol reporters with news announcements worth covering.

Responsibility for finding material for those press conferences fell to our press secretary, Tom Roeser. Don Padilla did not follow us into the governor's office. Elmer hired Roeser instead. A native of Illinois who had been educated at St. John's University in Collegeville, Minnesota, Tom was a thirty-two-year-old Republican Party publicist in 1961 who'd put in stints as U.S. Rep. Al Quie's press secretary, city editor of the *St. Cloud Times,* and reporter for the Associated Press. He eventually became a well-known conservative talk radio host in Chicago, a local version of Rush Limbaugh. Tom was smart, witty, and creative—a delightful person—but he was also excitable, somewhat disorganized, and a bit insecure. Elmer called him a "free spirit." Tom would complain that Elmer liked his State Patrol–assigned driver, Bob Eickstadt, more than him. Tom was given to fretting about such things. Then again, Elmer did think highly of Bob, and Tom seemed to attract trouble.

As a state senator, Elmer had sponsored the state's first major civil rights legislation in 1955. As governor, he was very interested in promoting racial justice and inclusivity. That made George Manser a favored staff member too. Manser was our staffer handling Indian affairs and was instrumental in arranging a gubernatorial tour of Minnesota's Indian reservations that Elmer thoroughly enjoyed. Elmer would praise Manser in Roeser's presence, fueling Tom's jealousy and paranoia. Roeser retaliated by nicknaming Manser "Little Lord Dumpling." He said it often enough that the name stuck. Before long, the entire Capitol was calling Manser "Dumpling," and I had a piqued staffer on my hands.

If Tom didn't have a news story ready for Elmer to bring to reporters at his twice-weekly news conferences, Elmer would grab almost anything off his desk and use it. He had a letter one week from a whistle-blowing disgruntled employee of insurance commissioner Cyrus Magnusson. Magnusson had been a Freeman appointee. (In those years, most state agency heads' terms of office did not coincide with the governor's. A new governor had only a few commissioners to appoint.) Elmer was short of material for his news conference, so he announced that his administration was looking at this charge. Within minutes, I had a call from an irate Magnusson. "What's this all about?" he exclaimed. I had to confess that I did not know and vowed that we would look into it. Roeser was in the doghouse for not providing better material to the governor. He would get so upset when that happened that a few times I thought he was having a heart attack in my office.

Tom and I traveled together to the 1961 National Governors Association meeting in Hawaii, which had just become a state and was attracting considerable national interest. As a gift to Eleanor for having endured the campaign, Elmer decided that they would travel to Hawaii by steamship. That left the Minnesota National Guard's Stratocruiser, a well-appointed four-engine plane, available for our use. We invited the governors of neighboring states that lacked such a plane to fly with us. I was tasked with orchestrating the travel and hospitality for four or five governors and their parties. We flew to San Francisco, spent a night there, then continued to Hawaii the next day. We became friendly with Wisconsin Gov. Gaylord Nelson and his outgoing, outspoken wife, Carrie Lee. She told us, "Gaylord gives me a quota of 100 votes a day that I can lose for him, and I never fail to meet my quota."

That night, the governor of Hawaii had a welcoming reception for the visiting governors and their delegations. Elmer had not arrived yet. We gravitated over to Carrie Nelson, who was having an animated conversation with someone. As we approached, we (and plenty of others) heard her respond to him with a tart "F*** that noise!" I turned to Tom Roeser and said, "Boy, I see what she meant about costing her husband votes."

Roeser was my roommate on that trip. He seemed to be in a constant state of chaos. He somehow lost both his wedding ring and his underwear. He went for a walk on the beach and came back with his pants wet up to his thighs.

"What happened to you?" I asked.

"A wave hit me," he said.

"How could a wave hit you up to your thighs?" He didn't have an answer.

With Tom, things sometimes didn't go as planned. One incident on the 1962 campaign trail stands out. It's one that Roeser himself related to a University of Minnesota audience at an observance of what would have been Elmer's one-hundredth birthday,

June 17, 2009. Tom and Elmer were traveling to the Marshall County Fair in Warren, Minnesota, in the northwestern corner of the state. Elmer had just seen poll numbers that had him neck and neck with DFL candidate Karl Rolvaag. That poll proved to be accurate. Elmer was a bit dispirited, and Tom was on his best behavior. He asked Elmer if there was anything he could do to help him at the fair where Elmer was to speak.

Elmer allowed that he would be grateful for Tom's attention to one detail. He would like a glass of water placed on the rostrum before he began to speak so that he could sip it during his remarks. That would spare him the need to repeatedly clear his throat as he spoke.

But at the county fair arena where Elmer was to speak, no rostrum had been placed on the stage. There was only a microphone on a stand. Tom got busy distributing press releases, while the crowd was entertained with a series of vaudeville acts—a singer, a juggler, a magician, and a high-wire act featuring a midget in red pantaloons and high black patent leather boots, riding on a tiny motorcycle. The acts ended abruptly, and it was Elmer's turn to speak. Tom had not found a glass of water for the boss, let alone decided where to put it. He ran to a refreshment stand outside the arena and got the water. Somehow he found a folding chair on which to place the glass. He decided to go to the back of the stage and approach someone seated on the stage's last row of seats. He'd ask if that person would unobtrusively set the chair and the glass of water close to the governor, in a spot where Elmer could see it. He stressed to the person he found that it was important not to make a great fuss, since the governor was in the middle of a serious speech.

Only after his recruited helper stood up did Tom realize that the person he had tapped for this assignment was the midget, still wearing red pantaloons and patent leather boots. Tom tried to summon him back, but the determined fellow was on his way, hauling a chair as big as he was and sloshing the water about. The crowd saw his effort before Elmer did and began tittering. Elmer eventually turned around, just in time for the midget to hand him a nearly empty glass of water. The crowd assumed this was part of the midget's act and cheered. But the campaign message Elmer was trying to convey was lost.

Soon and for years thereafter, Elmer would laugh about episodes such as that one. But at that time, in the middle of a tight election contest, the humor was lost on him. On the trip home from Marshall County, Tom Roeser didn't have to wonder what the governor thought of his performance that day. Elmer made his evaluation clear.

WHEN THE TERM OF OFFICE of the state commissioner of business development expired in late 1961, Elmer knew that he wanted a change. James W. Clark had held that post since the office was created nineteen years earlier, and he expected to be there forever. But Elmer wanted more vigor in that office. He considered the selling of Minnesota to potential investors, tourists, convention-goers, and residents to be among state government's most important functions. He wanted his own man in that post—me. I was a willing recruit. Milt Knoll, a former executive secretary for the Republican Party of Ramsey County who had been our legislative staffer, took over in the governor's office as chief of staff.

I shared Elmer's view that Minnesota could do a lot more to pick up the pace of both business and population growth, which were lagging the national average in the middle of the twentieth century. "An overall state plan for progress is needed," I said at the news conference at which Elmer announced my appointment. Part of that plan had to involve instilling a more positive attitude in the state's own residents. "Minnesota needs a heads-up, chin-up, chest-out attitude in selling the state and its wares." It was the same song I'd been singing since the centennial.

The commissioner's job brought me in contact with some of the state's business luminaries. For example, Curt Carlson, founder of the Carlson Companies and owner of Radisson Hotels, was a significant contributor to our tourism promotion advisory committee. Jack Madden—at whose Brainerd-area resort Arlene and I had spent our honeymoon—was involved too and became a good friend.

I was back on the public speaking circuit, touting the ideas that Minnesotans should brag about their state and communities should form economic development commissions and develop promotional strategies. We also took our pitch for Minnesota tourism to a half-dozen other major cities—Chicago, St. Louis, and several places in California were among them. Our gimmick was to rent a good-sized meeting room in hotels and set up a portable water tank, which we would stock with live fish furnished by the Minnesota Department of Natural Resources (DNR). One might say it was the road-show version of the State Fair DNR exhibit. We'd invite travel writers to come in and catch fish. It produced some great stories. I always worried that if the tank leaked or collapsed, we'd be responsible for a big, costly mess; fortunately, that didn't happen.

Elmer accompanied us on our trip to Chicago because it included a stop in Skokie at the headquarters of Bell & Howell, a maker of movie equipment. It was involved in a promotional project we were planning. Bell & Howell's CEO was Charles Percy, with whom Elmer was acquainted. Percy was active in Republican politics and had been one of the guest speakers at Minnesota's 1960 Republican convention. The two of them hit it off, in part because they had similar business backgrounds. Like Elmer at H. B. Fuller, Percy had gone to work for Bell & Howell as a young man, when it was a small company, and after taking charge as its CEO had overseen substantial growth.

At some point during our meeting, Percy turned to me and said, "Would you mind excusing yourself? I'd like to discuss something with Elmer." I bowed out and waited. Afterward, I asked Elmer for an explanation.

"He's thinking about running for office and wanted to get my advice," Elmer said. It occurred to me that Elmer was one of the few governors who had also built major businesses and could counsel Percy on making the transition from CEO to political candidate. In 1964, a tough year for Republicans, Percy ran unsuccessfully for governor of Illinois. He had more success in 1966, winning a U.S. Senate seat he would hold with distinction for twenty years.

We pursued a variety of ideas for attracting more visitors and businesses to Minnesota. One was to get celebrities to visit and talk about their happy vacations in the state. The creative people at the Campbell Mithun advertising agency in Minneapolis took that idea one step further: could we get the stars of Hollywood's famous

Road to . . . series of movies, Bob Hope and Bing Crosby, to do a "Road to Minnesota"? I don't know what magic they had at that ad agency, but they were able to get Hope and Crosby to perform a skit and song for a 45-rpm record about Minnesota as a vacation wonderland. It didn't cost the state's taxpayers a dime. The recording is full of corny jokes and references to lakes, loons, moose, and the fun of walking across the Mississippi River at its headwaters in Itasca State Park, all told by two of the most recognizable voices of the twentieth century. We distributed 20,000 copies at little cost to the taxpayer. Today that recording is a nice souvenir of a job I truly enjoyed but had to give up too soon.

CHAPTER 16

Recount

I WASN'T INVOLVED in Elmer's 1962 reelection campaign—at least not as a paid staff member. My role as commissioner of business development precluded me from taking an official position in the campaign. But I followed it closely, of course, and served as a sounding board and dispenser of advice to both the candidate and his aides.

That was close enough for me to feel jitters as the polls tightened and anger as Elmer's opponent, Lt. Gov. Karl Rolvaag, and his DFL allies distorted Elmer's record. In those years, Minnesota's governor and lieutenant governor ran independently. Rolvaag, the son of a well-known author and professor at St. Olaf College, had been lieutenant governor throughout Gov. Orville Freeman's six-year tenure. When the voters replaced Freeman with Andersen in 1960, they retained Rolvaag. By 1962, after eight years in the low-capacity lieutenant governor's office, Rolvaag was hungry to move up to the governorship. And the DFL Party, whose de facto head was my distant cousin, U.S. Sen. Hubert Humphrey, was willing to pull out all their stops to get him there.

The DFL onslaught culminated in political trickery. It was a classic October surprise—an accusation leveled in late October, during the campaign's waning days. Rolvaag's team claimed that Andersen had rushed the paving of an off-ramp on new Interstate 35 near Hinckley, despite weather too cold for the concrete to safely set, in order to complete the roadway and open it before the election. The whole thing was bogus. There was no flaw in the paving of that stretch of highway other than of the routine sort that the contractor repaired at his own expense for less than $1,000. The weather may have been cold the day the road was paved, as the DFLers said, but the ground was warm enough for paving, and that was what mattered. But a politician as adroit as Humphrey was undeterred by those facts. He found federal officials willing to say that the quality of I-35 construction in Minnesota was under review. That was the point Humphrey emphasized on statewide television on November 5, the night before the election, with Karl Rolvaag and Attorney General Walter Mondale at his side.

The stretch of highway in question had been formally opened with a ribbon-cutting event on the previous Thursday, November 1. Elmer was a featured speaker and made headlines with an angry defense of his administration's oversight of the road's construction. "I deeply resent the cheap, dirty politicians who, to get a few votes, have besmirched Minnesota's good name all over the country," he said. The next morning's newspapers described the governor's heated words at length.

For some reason, I accompanied Elmer two days later on a campaign stop in Anoka. Already Anoka was making a name for itself for its elaborate observance of Halloween and was an important campaign stop in any statewide campaign's closing days. Elmer wasn't happy that day. He berated himself for his performance at the highway dedication. He should have made fun of the DFL's crazy accusation, he moaned. He shouldn't have lost his temper. I tried to reassure him. I didn't agree that it was a mistake to flare up. The DFL machine—Humphrey, Rolvaag, U.S. Rep. John Blatnik, Mondale, and federal officials in Washington who were playing along—were grabbing the state's attention with their barrage. Until Thursday, attempts to counter their claims were playing behind the want ads in the state's daily newspapers. He had to speak sharply to get his side out, I told him. I'm not sure he believed me.

The night before the election, as the DFLers repeated their accusation on statewide television, I was in Wadena in northern Minnesota, addressing a county redevelopment group. I had a long drive home with the radio as my companion and an earful of campaign news to put me on edge. I remember thinking, "Thank God, this will be settled tomorrow." If only that had been true.

I MUST HAVE BEEN AT THE LEAMINGTON HOTEL with Elmer and Eleanor on election night, although I recall little about that long, inconclusive evening. The Andersens left the hotel at 4:00 A.M. thinking Elmer was ahead by a few hundred votes. That lead would slip away, then return, several times over the next forty-eight to seventy-two hours. Reports about counting irregularities began to arrive as well. The election had ended in what amounted to a draw. Rolvaag's attorney Sydney Berde quickly went to some counties to ask boards of commissioners to recanvass, or recount, the ballots in places where errors seemed obvious. We picked up on that idea, approaching more counties than he did. Then Berde went to court to oppose our implementation of his strategy. It became clear that it wouldn't do to have a recount only in places where one party or the other saw a chance for gain. A statewide recount was in order.

When the campaign team huddled a few days after the election, I was invited to sit in. Elmer asked me to be his recount manager. It would mean a taking a leave of absence—or leaving—the business development commissioner's job.

"I don't have any experience with recounts," I responded.

"We've quickly established that no one does," Elmer replied. "You're it."

I mumbled something about promising Arlene that I would paint our bedroom. David Lilly, the campaign's finance chair, countered that he'd hire someone to paint our bedroom—which he did, for $175.

I couldn't say no. The understanding was that I would be granted a leave of absence from the Department of Business Development. If Elmer prevailed in the election, I'd return to the commissioner's post. If he didn't, I wouldn't want to return.

Elmer was declared the winner by 142 votes when the state Canvassing Board met on November 26. But he had already announced that he would support Rolvaag's call for a recount regardless of the count at the Canvassing Board. He believed that the state needed the clarity a recount would provide. It would involve representatives of both campaigns watching as election judges sorted and counted paper ballots, and challenging, or referring to the judicial system for review, any ballots we believed were counted in error.

We decided to stipulate the accuracy of counts obtained in places that used voting machines, which were used in Minneapolis,

St. Paul, and only a few other places in Hennepin and Ramsey counties. Nearly three-fourths of the nearly 1.3 million votes cast were on paper ballots. That decision gave Rolvaag an inherent advantage. Then and now, Minneapolis and St. Paul voted heavily DFL. Republican voters were more numerous in the rest of the state. That meant we had greater exposure to errors. Our only chance to win was to get every possible paper vote counted in our favor.

We needed a strong legal team to help us handle the litigation that is an inevitable part of any recount. Elmer suggested that we consider using his personal attorney, Samuel Morgan of the Briggs and Morgan firm in St. Paul. I met with him, but we determined his expertise didn't align well with this assignment. His two partners were Richard Kyle and J. Neil Morton. Dick had been a high-ranking military officer in World War II and possessed a take-charge personality. His nickname was "the General." Neil was more reserved. Both were extraordinary guys. Neither had been much involved in politics, but their strong reputation as litigators persuaded me they should be our team. I went to their office to sell them on the idea. They were a bit late and arrived wearing somber faces, having just attended a funeral together. I was surprised to learn that despite years in the same firm, they'd never worked together on a case. They were willing to make the recount their first joint assignment.

Kyle and Morton helped us decide our recount strategy: challenge any ballot bearing a stray mark of any kind—an erasure, a write-in, a scribble, you name it. "If they voted for Rolvaag and there's a flyspeck on the ballot, challenge it." That's the word I spread in our one and only briefing session for about one hundred volunteer recounters. We recruited them with the help of the Republican Party and GOP-leaning law firms. We wanted people with sharp eyes, quick reflexes, and little reticence. That's why our preference was for people under the age of fifty.

The counting did not begin until December 20. There were mistakes galore. That's understandable, given that paper ballots were hand-counted on election night by election judges who had already been on the job all day and were often still at it after midnight. Reports from our counters poured into our headquarters on the second floor of The St. Paul Hotel. It was a stressful time as a small group of us deployed people all over the state. One of our lieutenants needled me for years thereafter about being a Scrooge of a boss, giving the team Christmas morning off and asking them to come to the office that afternoon. That was the intensity of our work.

By the time the recount was complete a few weeks later, 97,000 of 1,267,502 ballots had been challenged by either Rolvaag's team or ours. We went that far because the state's election laws in those years were vague and imprecise. There was another recount in Minnesota that year, in state House District Twelve in Scott County, that proceeded through the courts a few weeks ahead of ours. DFL state Rep. John Fitzgerald and his Republican challenger, Henry Morlock, were in a near dead heat that went first to a recount, then to the district court, and finally to the Supreme Court. Morlock won by ten votes. The legal decisions in that case set precedents that helped shrink the number of challenged ballots in our case to a more manageable number.

AS OUR RECOUNT MOVED into the litigation phase, the impartiality of the Minnesota judiciary to deal with all those challenged ballots was called into question by nationally syndicated columnist Drew Pearson—whom I suspect was relying on tips planted by Hubert Humphrey. Supreme Court Chief Justice Oscar Knutson was furious. (He was a crusty fellow from Warren, in northwestern Minnesota. Elmer had promoted him from associate to chief justice. I learned from him that my mother had taught him to dance while he was a student at the boarding high school that today is the University of Minnesota Crookston.) Knutson called the two legal teams, including me, into his chambers. "I don't want to see this thing again," he told us. He directed us to go into a room and not to come out until we had decided on the names of three district court judges acceptable to both sides who would adjudicate the recount's legal issues. We weren't to worry about recruiting them—he'd take care of that. "Short of them being on their deathbeds, I'll get them to serve to finish this thing," Knutson said.

Our lawyers and theirs—Clayton Nelson, Bob Breunig, and Mary Lou Klas—retired to an evening of more frank conversation about this state's judges than I ever heard before or since. I could contribute little, but I listened in fascination. The names we settled on were Sidney Kaner of Duluth, J. H. Sylvestre of Crookston, and Leonard J. Keyes Jr. of St. Paul. That lineup was supposed to be politically neutral. Kaner has been a DFLer, appointed by DFL Gov. Orville Freeman; Sylvestre had been a Republican, appointed by Gov. Luther Youngdahl; and Len Keyes had come to the bench by being elected a municipal judge during Freeman's years. Elmer had allowed local bar associations to make recommendations via plebiscite to fill district judicial slots. That process led to Elmer promoting Keyes to the district court. That history supposedly made him beholden to both parties—but later, Keyes told me, "If my father ever thought I was anything other than a died-in-the-wool Democrat, he'd turn over in his grave."

I give Elmer immense credit for not interfering with the recount or the subsequent legal proceedings in any way. He was intent on doing the best job he could as governor as long as he was the occupant of the office. He didn't bother us. If it had been me in that position, I think I would have been calling in every hour asking how the count was going. By all accounts, Rolvaag was heavily involved. But he didn't have a state to run.

Elmer did, and that included correcting a problem on the state Supreme Court. Chief Justice Knutson had come to him seeking help. Associate Justice Frank Gallagher, a member of a large DFL-leaning family, was seventy-five years old and showing his age. Knutson asked Elmer to try to convince Gallagher to retire. Elmer did by telling Gallagher that he would appoint in his stead a highly regarded former Liberal Caucus legislator from Mankato, Robert Sheran, a law partner of Gallagher's brother. Elmer knew the appointment would make waves. He came to our office at The St. Paul Hotel the day before he made the announcement to brief me on his intention. "This is the most important thing a governor does," Elmer said by way of explanation. I give him credit for giving me advance notice so I could be prepared for the reaction that followed.

Sheran would go on to become one of the most respected jurists in state history, but that wasn't how Sheran was perceived on January 8, when Elmer made his appointment official. Elmer didn't reveal until he wrote his 2000 autobiography that choosing Sheran was an inducement to get Gallagher to retire. All that was known in 1963 was that in the middle of a contentious recount, when hundreds of Republican volunteers were busting their tails to help get a Republican governor reelected, that same governor appointed a DFLer to a coveted seat on the Supreme Court. Some of the people who were working on the recount blew their stacks. "What does this guy think he's doing? Doesn't he know what it means to be the leader of his party?" they said.

I regretted their disappointment. I had developed great respect for the people we worked with on the recount. That's true not only of our own team but the other side as well. Those DFLers were fine people. Mary Lou Klas became the first woman appointed to the Ramsey County District Court in 1986. Harold Kalina also became a judge, and later chief judge, of the Hennepin County District Court. Clayton Nelson was a plainspoken country lawyer from New Prague and a very honorable guy. Robert Breunig became a district court judge in Dakota County and served for twenty-four years. Together we learned that election judges make mistakes, that paper ballots are error-prone, and that voter education is necessary so that most voters come to the polls knowing what to expect and how to cast a ballot. Those lessons informed the legislators who set future state election law.

Among the points of contention: what to do about a paper ballot to which a voter had signed his name in violation of state law? That error had been committed by a first-time voter in Stearns County. As he was leaving the voting booth, he heard one election judge say to another, "Did you initial the ballots?" An election judge's initials are required to authenticate paper ballots. The young man thought the judge was speaking to him, not to another judge, and thought that if initials were desired, a full signature would be even better. That signature sent him outside Stearns County for the first time in his life and landed him before our three-judge panel as it considered whether challenged ballots would be counted. The young man's story convinced the judges to accept his ballot as valid. That gave one more vote to Rolvaag. As the young voter prepared to step down from the witness stand, Judge Sylvestre said to him, "Don't be discouraged about voting. I can assure you, this isn't what happens every time you vote!"

As the three judges whittled down the stack of challenged ballots, it was evident that we were losing ground. Finally, on March 15, the counting ended at 619,842 for Rolvaag, 619,751 for Andersen. That ninety-one-vote margin was the closest gubernatorial election in Minnesota history.

We were allowed to file a few motions and a final plea. Its gist was that any election that takes this long and is this contested and winds up this close is one whose winner cannot be known with certainty. On that basis, and given the time that had elapsed, Elmer should continue as governor. It was a weak argument, and we knew it. On March 20, the three-judge panel declared Rolvaag the winner of the election. Elmer had a few days in which to decide whether to appeal that decision to the state Supreme Court or to concede and turn the governor's office over to Rolvaag.

That night, Elmer, Morton, Kyle, and I met in the third-floor dining room of the St. Paul Athletic Club. Elmer had never experienced an election defeat before. He was under heavy pressure from state Republican leaders to press on with legal appeals. We counseled him gently but clearly. There's no sound legal basis for an appeal, the lawyers said. One could be filed that might keep him in office through the end of the 1963 legislative session, but it would not lead to a different outcome, and it would be seen as a spurious delaying tactic. I shared my sense that an appeal would be viewed negatively by the great mass of the public.

He had the weekend to consider his options. He didn't take that much time. He called a news conference on Saturday afternoon, March 23, to announce that on Monday, March 25, Karl Rolvaag would become the state's thirty-first governor. His remarks that day were so eloquent that at the urging of many who were present, they were printed in pamphlet form and widely distributed. "I am disappointed but not the least discouraged; I am defeated but not the least disheartened. I am deeply grateful to the people of Minnesota for the privilege that has been mine to serve as governor of this great state. . . . Our family is united. Our love has deepened and broadened through this experience, we are thankful we have retained good health, and we continue to be humbly grateful for the rich blessings of God that we have so abundantly received."

Elmer's service to Minnesota was far from over. He went on to chair the University of Minnesota Board of Regents, preside over the Minnesota Historical Society, play a key role in the passage of the Taconite Amendment in 1964 and in the founding of Voyageurs National Park in the 1970s, and much more. He also built his company, H. B. Fuller, to national status and founded another company, ECM Publishing. He was an extraordinary contributor to this state. When he died on November 15, 2004, at the age of ninety-five, no former governor was more beloved.

As for me, I had recount bills to pay, an office to shut down, and a job to find. The cost to the state's taxpayers of this exercise in democracy was $225,000. It was a bargain. I enjoyed public service, but decided again—as I had in 1959—that my family would be better served by the opportunities and stability that the private sector offered. Arlene and I took the family on an overdue vacation trip to Washington, DC, and Williamsburg, Virginia. Then I accepted a position at the St. Paul Fire and Marine Insurance Co.

CHAPTER 17

Insurance Man

I JOINED ST. PAUL FIRE AND MARINE INSURANCE to replace the firm's retiring public relations director. That was the first of a series of positions I held at the firm that would take the name The St. Paul Companies in 1968. It was my professional home for twenty-three years, longer than I spent working anywhere else.

Ron Hubbs was part of the cement that attached me to The St. Paul Companies. He was a wonderful man, gracious and even-tempered, who succeeded Archie Jackson as CEO shortly after I arrived. He took corporate leadership very seriously and genuinely valued the work of the public relations (later, communications) office. He insisted that every statement issued to employees or the public over his name be crafted with great care.

That was driven home to me on November 22, 1963, when President John F. Kennedy was assassinated. It was a Friday afternoon when the tragic word reached St. Paul from Dallas, causing great consternation, apprehension, and sorrow among our employees. This was the height of the Cold War. No one knew initially whether the attack on the president was the act of a lone gunman or a conspiracy by the nation's Soviet enemies. Had it been the latter, it could have meant nuclear war.

Hubbs called me seeking advice. What should we say or do? he asked. I asked for a moment to think about it, then called my counterpart at 3M, the largest private employer in the eastern half of the metro area. He was puzzling over the same thing. We decided to tell each of our CEOs to send a telegram to our two U.S. senators, Hubert Humphrey and Eugene McCarthy, expressing concern and pledging help, whatever that might entail. Then we'd ask the CEOs to use their corporate public address systems to tell employees about the message they'd sent. The message didn't carry much substance, but it seemed to be asserting leadership and that would be reassuring just then. I proposed that plan to Hubbs. He quickly agreed and asked me to prepare a statement he could read to employees. The statement I wrote and brought to him a few minutes later included the phrase "this outrageous act" in reference to the assassination.

"Tom, isn't 'outrageous' a little strong?" he said.

"Ron, if this incident doesn't warrant 'outrageous,' nothing does," I replied. He thought a second more, then agreed.

My job included writing speeches for him, which got the same careful review. He'd sometimes object when a speech employed repetition to drive home a point.

"People generally don't remember what you said before," I assured him. "Repetition is often necessary to get one's message across." I'm not sure I completely sold him on that notion, but he kept using the speeches I wrote.

Insurance is about managing risk. Ron's way of managing risk in his personal life was to avoid it. He wasn't quick to adapt to change. When the Interstate 94 links to and from downtown St. Paul were young but no longer brand-new, it fell to me one day to drive the company car, a Buick, to Minneapolis. My passengers were Ron and his predecessor Archie Jackson, then the chair of the corporate board. I knew a quick route to the freeway that involved a right turn. As soon as I turned, Ron piped up, "You're going the wrong way."

"Let him drive—he knows what he's doing," Archie assured.

Ron wasn't convinced until he saw for himself that my route worked. It spared us two stop signs. It was a revelation to Ron, and he was always pleased to learn something new. "Why didn't somebody tell me before how to do this!" he exclaimed.

ST. PAUL FIRE AND MARINE INSURANCE proudly boasted that it is Minnesota's oldest company, founded in 1853. But changes in the insurance industry in the 1960s positioned it for a new identity. Ron called me in July 1968 with a daunting and somewhat mysterious assignment. One of our small subsidiaries was called the St. Paul Insurance Company. It sold insurance just in Minnesota, the only state in which it was licensed. Ron's instructions were to get the

St. Paul Insurance Company licensed in every state before the end of the year.

I asked him why.

"I can't tell you," he replied. "But we must get it done."

I'd been handed a Herculean assignment. It meant making formal legal applications to the insurance commissions of forty-nine states within about six months.

The head of our Insurance Law Department, Kernel Armbruster, reported to me. He had just begun a two-week vacation on the Gunflint Trail in Minnesota's remote Arrowhead region. I reached him by phone and told him to cancel the remainder of his vacation and come home. "Whaddaya mean?" he hollered. I explained, and his complaints subsided only a little. "That's impossible!" he said of our orders. I must have felt some sympathy for him. He talked me into cutting his vacation to one week.

We did not learn why we had been asked to undertake this huge endeavor until four months later. St. Paul Fire and Marine was a company restricted by law to selling insurance. It could offer no other financial services. That made us potential prey for the corporate conglomerates that were then emerging nationally. They were growing fast and generally in quest of quick capital. They often sought to acquire old-line, capital-rich property and liability insurance companies. We filled that bill, but we had no interest in being swallowed by any other entity. Our leadership decided that St. Paul Fire and Marine would become a general business corporation called The St. Paul Companies. We aimed to repel the conglomerates by becoming a multiline insurer positioned for further diversification. Our subsidiaries took on new purposes to adjust to the new corporate structure, which necessitated the St. Paul Insurance Company being admitted in every state in the union.

We had a good reputation, which helped us get our assignment done by year's end. The threat of a hostile takeover diminished. But our corporate leaders still fretted about that possibility. I was assigned to prepare a public relations defense for a takeover, just in case it was needed. The St. Paul Fire & Marine Insurance Company had registered its own stock, which meant that we knew the names and addresses of our stockholders. We could contact them on short notice if a takeover bid was mounted. We identified our principal stockholders and prepared a plan of action, right down to particular corporate executives calling particular stockholders with tailored appeals to resist any offer to buy us. We had a message roughly sketched out that could be refined and employed on short notice. In those days, 85 percent of our owners were either individuals or bank-managed trust accounts; only 15 percent were mutual funds or pension funds. We could craft our message to appeal to individual investors, not professional fund managers who demand constant returns. (In the ensuing twenty years, that stock ownership picture would almost completely reverse.)

There were a couple of nibbles from potential predators, but fortunately nothing materialized on my watch. Our effort to retain our independence worked. I was soon executive vice president, responsible for underwriting, human resources, marketing, communications, and government affairs.

THE ST. PAUL COMPANIES WERE MAJOR PLAYERS in the nation's property and casualty insurance industry. That is one of the reasons that I was chosen in 1981 to chair the Insurance Information Institute, a public information arm of the industry to which all of the nation's major capital stock insurance companies contributed. The institute was a valued source of information about an industry whose products were coming under increasing scrutiny in those years.

For example, medical malpractice insurance costs were skyrocketing, for a number of reasons. The growth of large group medical practices weakened the personal connection between doctors and patients. New drugs and surgical procedures were being introduced rapidly, sometimes before all of their risks were known. The biggest factor boosting prices may have been what the industry called "social and economic inflation." Americans were becoming more litigious and jury awards more generous, especially as the nation endured high rates of inflation in the late 1970s.

The St. Paul Companies was then the largest provider of medical malpractice insurance in the country. Our policies were "occurrence contracts." Any medical procedure in a given year that resulted in a claim by a patient would be covered, no matter when that claim was made. Often claims were reported years after the procedure in question. Pricing a medical malpractice insurance contract was extremely difficult. Many insurance companies got out of the business in those years, contending that medical malpractice was uninsurable.

We didn't know the extent to which medical malpractice was hurting us until we hired our first actuary. For years, our company had operated without its own actuary, the specialized mathematicians who determine how insurance policies should be priced. We relied on information provided by actuaries in the industry associations. Our first in-house actuary was Gus Oien. Actuaries are sometimes stereotyped as mathematically gifted but verbally challenged. That may be an unfair generalization for an entire profession, but it aptly described Gus.

One day Gus came to Bill King, our chief underwriting officer, to inform him that our medical malpractice insurance loss reserves were $25 million short. Bill came to us in the executive suite to report the bad news. We could scarcely believe it. Are you sure? How could that be? Would you check again? It was totally out of corporate character for The St. Paul Companies to operate with insufficient reserves. We finally conceded that Oien's figures were solid and that CEO Carl Drake needed to know.

Drake had succeeded Hubbs in 1973. He was another excellent leader, a man of great integrity, good sense, and gracious manners. It wasn't typical of him to use strong language. But when Gus finally got out the message that our medical malpractice loss reserves were $25 million short, Drake exploded in a totally uncharacteristic way.

"Oien, you're full of shit!" he exclaimed.

Oien countered with a remarkably lucid reply: "Mr. Drake, I may be full of shit. But you're still short $25 million." He was right.

Our corporate leadership concluded that the only way we could afford to stay in the business was to move away from occurrence contracts. We decided to switch from "occurrence" to "claims made." We would agree to cover a physician or hospital for all the claims made in a given year, regardless of when the procedure or treatment in question was performed. But we would not cover future claims reported about that year's work—unless, of course, the physician in question was still a policyholder in that future year as well. We also offered physicians a guarantee that we would not drop their coverage from one year to the next, as long as they stayed with us. That change allowed us to base premium prices on more predictable current-year claims.

Our Insurance Law Department had the responsibility of assuring that insurance commissioners in all the states in which we sold malpractice insurance approved the change to a claims-made contract. I was significantly involved in selling that change. Most doctors didn't like this, of course. And doctors tend to have friends in high political places. We took a lot of heat, including the Maryland Legislature telling us that if we didn't continue with occurrence contracts, the state wouldn't let us sell insurance of any kind in the state. The states of New York and Michigan never accommodated us. But the change eventually went forward in most places, keeping us in the medical malpractice business and keeping doctors and hospitals insured.

COMPANY POLICY REQUIRED RETIREMENT at age sixty-five. That came for me in 1986. Drake's tenure ended not long before mine; Robert J. Haugh was CEO when I stepped down.

It was my privilege during my twenty-three-year tenure at The St. Paul Companies to be associated with top-flight CEOs—Archie Jackson, Ron Hubbs, Carl Drake, Waverly Smith, Bob Haugh. Each was committed to expanding, improving, and strengthening the company. That was their priority. Self-enrichment was never their aim. They were great role models for me and everyone else who worked with them.

One kindness the company showed me continues to this day. I've maintained an office at their expense, first in-house, then across the street at the Landmark Center, now back in the corporate building. That office has been a great asset to me through what is now twenty-eight years of postretirement civic work—more years than I spent in the company's employ. I pay for parking, but for most of that time, I've paid no rent for the office itself. My office mates for a time were my former bosses Ron Hubbs and Carl Drake and retired senior executive vice president Bob Davis—a congenial group. For many years our assistant was Emily Gieske, who gave us marvelous support.

In 2004, The St. Paul Companies acquired Travelers Insurance of Hartford, Connecticut, to form the nation's second-largest commercial property and liability insurance company. The St. Paul name was retained for a little more than two years afterward, then dropped in favor of the better-known name Travelers. The company still has operations in downtown St. Paul and is incorporated in Minnesota, but its headquarters has moved to New York. I count that change as a net loss for this state.

I HAD THE HONOR of delivering the eulogies at the funerals of both Ron Hubbs and his wife Margaret, who died in 2013 at age ninety-nine. She'd had a crippling stroke the year before, and her doctor and son told her she could simply accept her disability and spend the rest of her days quietly, or she could undertake rigorous therapy to try to recover lost function. "It'll be a terrible fight," they warned her. She thought for a moment, then said, "I want to fight." She progressed sufficiently to leave the hospital and return to her home at Episcopal Homes before she died. I admired that. She was a great lady.

CHAPTER 18

Minnesota's Favorite Son

I DIDN'T LEAVE POLITICS COMPLETELY BEHIND when I left state service. I had become an active Republican during my years with Elmer. I was involved with the Republican Workshop, and for a time spent one night per week as a facilitator of its meetings. It was a national organization aimed at selling the Republican Party. One Minnesotan, Mary Hoffman, became its national president.

Another active member was Mamie Green, an African American woman then in her sixties who lived in St. Paul. Mamie recruited me to meet with a St. Paul African American group at her home to try to sell them on Republican principles and candidates. Her invitation came with one caveat: "Remember, Tom, most of these will be elderly people. They don't like to be out late at night. You'll have to wrap things up by 9:00 P.M." I assured her that would be no problem.

We had several sessions. I don't think any of them ended before 11:00 P.M. It was 1964, and the civil rights movement was in full swing. Arizona Sen. Barry Goldwater's presidential candidacy was becoming a rallying point for Americans who didn't like the civil rights movement. Meanwhile, Minnesota Sen. Hubert Humphrey was leading the Senate's historic struggle to enact the landmark 1964 Civil Rights Act.

As it became clear that Goldwater would be the party's nominee in 1964, my chances of convincing African Americans in St. Paul to vote a straight Republican ticket dwindled sharply. But I give Mamie's guests credit for showing up and discussing their concerns with such sincerity. They weren't ready to give up on the Republican Party. I wish more unhappy Republicans had exhibited that spirit that year. Mamie and I became friends, and she was my nominator to serve on the GOP State Executive Committee. Her support was a point of pride for me.

MY BIG EFFORT—or so I thought—on the executive committee would be internal party reform. In those years, Greater Minnesota had a disproportionate share of seats on the GOP state central committee. I made it my project to get that changed.

But 1964 was a pivotal time for the party nationally, and I couldn't let my focus be purely local. The long-moribund anti–New Deal right wing of the GOP was coming back to life. In Goldwater, it had found a champion. Heir to a department store fortune, Goldwater rejected New Deal ideas about government stimulus of the economy and a federal responsibility for social welfare. He also resisted federal efforts to impose racial equality and advocated a hawkish stance against communism and the Soviet Union.

Some of us in Minnesota Republican circles were concerned about Goldwater. We thought his brand of conservatism was too extreme. Compared with today's Republicans, he'd be considered moderate, or maybe even liberal. But in 1964, he was an alarming figure. For president, we much preferred Elmer Andersen's good friend, New York Gov. Nelson Rockefeller. When "Rocky" lost the crucial California primary to Goldwater, giving the Arizona senator a lock on the presidential nomination, the party's progressive leaders in Ramsey and Hennepin Counties huddled to consider our options. We wanted to separate our state party from the national debacle for Republicans that we feared a Goldwater candidacy would bring.

We were a sizable group. In St. Paul, it included Harry Strong, Harry Weisbecker, Frank Claiborne, and Frank Farrell; in Minneapolis, our group included Sally Pillsbury, John McGrory, Lyall Schwarzkopf, and Wayne Popham. (Sally's brother Wheelock Whitney was the party's U.S. Senate candidate that year against Democratic Sen. Eugene McCarthy.) We met at the old Ambassador hotel in St. Louis Park. One of us counseled that we shouldn't go to the national convention just being opposed to Goldwater. We should be for somebody, some plausible alternative candidate who stood for the principles we favored. McGrory said, "Let's try Walter Judd and see if he will be our favorite-son candidate."

Walter Judd was a politician of lofty principle and internationalist inclination whom many in our group had admired for decades. A physician, he spent two stints over a total of ten years as a medical missionary in China before running for Congress in 1942. He represented the Minneapolis-dominated Fifth Congressional District for twenty years, becoming a leading voice on foreign affairs. He lost his seat in 1962 when redistricting and the city's shift in political allegiance toward the DFL cost him his political base. Many of his people held Elmer and me accountable for the 1961 redistricting plan that preceded his defeat, but Elmer maintained that by 1961 there was no way to draw a Minneapolis congressional district that a Republican could win. Judd was succeeded by DFLer Don Fraser, who picked up where Judd left off as an advocate for peace and human rights in foreign affairs.

We contacted Judd, and he said, "Sure!" He shared our worry about Goldwater's hawkish attitude toward the Soviets and allowed that he still had some things he'd like to say to his country. Being a favorite-son candidate would give him a brief moment back in the spotlight.

Next, we had to convince the party faithful to elect national convention delegates willing to vote for Judd, not Goldwater. That led to some spirited contests. At the convention for the Fourth District, which in those years included Ramsey and Washington counties, the Judd faction's candidate was Ben Pomeroy, the dean of the University of Minnesota School of Veterinary Medicine and Ramsey County Republican chair. His Goldwater-backing opponent was Hugh Andersen of the Andersen Windows family. Pomeroy won, and in the interest of party unity, Hugh was made an alternate delegate.

Our group told Ben, "When you attend the convention proceedings, we want you to control your bodily functions so that you never have to leave the floor. We don't want Hugh Andersen coming down from the balcony and being seated." Ben was a fine gentleman who wasn't accustomed to coaching about such matters. But he took it in stride. When he came home, he proudly reported to our group, "I did it!"

I stayed home and watched as the twenty-six-member Minnesota delegation took its place on the floor of the Cow Palace in San Francisco in mid-July. The delegation's division was eighteen for Judd, eight for Goldwater. It was a pretty good reflection of sentiment among rank-and-file Republicans around the state. Most weren't ready for the lurch to the right that Goldwater represented. The state party made its independence very clear at the convention. But our jitters were renewed a few weeks later when President Lyndon Johnson chose Hubert Humphrey as his running mate. A Democratic landslide was coming. We hoped that our convention strategy would help spare Minnesota Republican candidates from the wave.

It did. Minnesota had four Republican congressmen in 1964—Al Quie, Ancher Nelson, Clark MacGregor, and Odin Langen—and all were reelected. I like to think that the stand we took in Minnesota helped those four establish an identity apart from Goldwater and stay in good graces with their constituents. By contrast, all six of Iowa's Republican congressmen were defeated in 1964.

The nation's historians point to the Goldwater candidacy as the beginning of what would be a major shift to the right in the Republican Party in the last decades of the twentieth century. In Minnesota, some Goldwater backers went home discouraged after 1964 and didn't return. But many came to see that you have to work together to succeed in politics. They learned to compromise and became positive contributors to the state party. As a result, Minnesota's GOP was slower than the rest of the country to make a hard right turn—though, to my regret, it finally did.

CHAPTER 19

St. Paul School Independence

I HAD BEEN WITH ST. PAUL FIRE AND MARINE Insurance Co. for less than a year when St. Paul League of Women Voters president and future city council member Ruby Hunt approached CEO Ron Hubbs. She wanted his blessing to ask me to cochair a campaign to convert St. Paul into an independent school district. The other cochair she had in mind was Howard Guthmann, a civic-minded tax accountant and Jaycee leader. Howard is my tax guy. I knew he'd do a fine job and that I would enjoy working with him.

Hubbs told her that The St. Paul Companies' policy was to encourage employees to be involved in public service. "But they have to get their jobs done first. That part is up to Swain." I took the school campaign responsibility with that understanding.

For years, public education had been the fiefdom of a designated member of the city council. In fact, between 1914 and 1950, St. Paul had no board of education at all. The city council controlled the schools. The council operated on a weak mayor, commission basis in those years, with each council member also heading a department of local government. That put the public schools on the same footing as the police and fire departments and public works. It led to some untenable political meddling in teacher hiring and compensation and in November 1946 to the first teachers' strike in the nation. As a new state senator in 1949, Elmer Andersen was involved in the initial move to wrest control of the schools from the city council. He and other reformers succeeded in reestablishing a board of education in 1950. It had operating authority over the schools, but the board was not yet financially independent from the council, and it couldn't levy taxes on its own authority. That was the aim of the referendum campaign Hunt was organizing. The referendum had two parts: to allow the school board to levy future school property taxes without the city council's permission, and to increase the existing levy for one year only, 1965. Without that increase, the district was facing the probability of budget cuts in the coming year.

Understandably, there was great skepticism on the part of the city's large Catholic community about these measures. Catholic schools served a sizable share of St. Paul families. Today the Archdiocese of St. Paul and Minneapolis operates the state's fourth-largest school system, behind Anoka-Hennepin, St. Paul, and Minneapolis public schools. It likely was the state's third largest a half century ago. Families sending their children to Catholic schools were already paying twice for education, via tuition and property taxes. They were fearful that if the school district were independent, school levies would climb with little direct benefit to their families.

The indirect benefit for them and for the next generation of St. Paul residents would be substantial, we argued. If the city's public schools were stronger, the whole region would be better for it—economically, culturally, and socially. But that wasn't the only message Catholic voters were hearing. The other came most forcefully from the referenda's leading opponents, the city's realtors. They feared that higher school taxes would mean fewer home sales and smaller incomes for them.

Mayor George Vavoulis was a vocal supporter of our Vote Yes/Yes campaign. We had a distinguished panel of civic and business leaders backing us too. But Howard and I concluded that we also needed a respected Catholic leader to affirm our argument and help sell it. We decided to pay a visit to the Rev. Msgr. James Shannon, president of what was then the College of St. Thomas in St. Paul, and ask for his endorsement.

Shannon was a bright rising star in Catholic circles. Just a few months older than me, he was a native of South St. Paul, a labor-dominated meatpacking town whose children often gained an affinity for working people and sympathy for the poor. He was a product of Catholic schools, graduating top of his class at both Cretin High School and the College of St. Thomas. He would be ordained a bishop one year after our school campaign and in 1968 would attract attention throughout this country and the Vatican when he resigned in protest of the papal encyclical forbidding the use of artificial birth control. He would go on to be a husband, a lawyer, a newspaper columnist, and a much-admired executive director of the Minneapolis Foundation and later the General Mills Foundation. In 1964, he was busy modernizing the all-male College of St. Thomas, starting it on a path that would eventually lead to coeducation, university status, and a national reputation for academic quality.

We gave Shannon our best pitch. He listened thoughtfully, then said, "I'm sorry, I can't publicly endorse your campaign. But I think I can do something equally effective." He wrote a letter to the archdiocesan newspaper, the *Catholic Bulletin*, which they published shortly before the election. In it, he said, in the final analysis, private and independent schools will only be as good as their neighboring public schools are. The public schools set the bar, and if that bar is too low, private schools will lag as well.

Shannon's argument worked. His letter got a lot of attention, making headlines in the October 30 *St. Paul Dispatch* newspaper. When the votes were counted the evening of November 3, both questions on the ballot were approved by narrow margins.

The next day, I was headed to a meeting at the St. Paul Athletic Club. Outside the entrance, I encountered three or four realtors with whom I was slightly acquainted. They stopped me and gave me hell for getting Shannon to write that letter. I'd had a back-and-forth in the press with the St. Paul Board of Realtors in the days before the election, as the realtors' group spread misinformation to try to defeat the referenda. They were convinced that the two questions would not have passed without Shannon's endorsement and that houses in St. Paul would be harder to sell with the higher property tax burden that had just been approved. I didn't stop then to argue with them, but today, I would. Real estate values are directly linked to the quality of public schools. The voters who owned homes had done themselves a favor.

HOWARD GUTHMANN AND I weren't through working together—and I don't mean on my tax returns. Thirty years after the school campaign, he and I were together again on the founding board of the Elder Learning Institute—today's Osher Lifelong Learning Institute, or OLLI. When I became its second president, he was our financial officer.

CHAPTER 20

Missing in Action

YOU KNOW THE OLD BROMIDE, "Lightning doesn't strike the same place twice"? Don't try telling that to the Swains. We don't believe it—not after 1968.

Arlene's husband and my friend Don Garniss was lost in 1944 when his B-24 plane went down off the coast of France. Because no one saw what happened, he was officially "missing in action." After one year, he was declared "killed in action." That settled the matter under the law and allowed Arlene to pursue a new life.

My stepdaughter Jo Anne never knew her father. Still, when Don's plane fell, Jo Anne's life changed. It couldn't happen twice, we all thought in early 1967 as we bade farewell to her handsome new twenty-four-year-old husband, Marine Capt. Patrick P. Murray. He was a navigator-bombardier with the 533rd All-Weather Tactical Squadron, which flew bombing missions over North Vietnam.

Patrick was the only child of a St. Paul barber, Ed Murray, and his wife, Jo, who worked for the St. Paul Department of Public Health. Pat and Jo Anne met when she was a senior in high school. They were sufficiently smitten with each other that their separation— while he was at the College of St. Thomas in St. Paul and she was a freshman at the University of Wisconsin–Madison—was fraught with lovesick misery. After that year, Jo Anne persuaded us that she should transfer to the University of Minnesota.

It's fair to say that any young man who pursues an eldest daughter does not win instant affection from a father, and it's fair to say that I was typical in that regard. But Pat worked his way into the hearts of the whole family. He taught Barbara how to parallel park so she could pass her driver's license exam, even letting her practice with his prized GTO sports car. He paid special attention to Mary and Spike, inspiring twelve-year-old Spike to get a memorably unbecoming military-style buzz haircut. Pat impressed Arlene with impeccable manners and devotion to his parents. He had chosen St. Thomas because it enabled him to stay close to home.

His respect for parents and tradition extended to me. After he proposed to Jo Anne, he came to the house on a Sunday afternoon to ask me for her hand the old-fashioned way. I may have been oblivious to the purpose of his request to meet with me—or maybe not. But when he appeared during the first half of a televised Minnesota Vikings football game, I stalled. "Wait until halftime," I said. That response cost me a lot of points with the rest of the household.

Arlene and I prevailed on Pat and Jo Anne not to marry until she graduated, which she did in December 1966. By then, Patrick was an ROTC graduate of St. Thomas and a naval flight officer in the Marine Corps based in Cherry Point, North Carolina.

They planned a December 31 wedding. There's a side story to that celebration. When I was in the governor's office in the early 1960s, the route and exit ramps for Interstate 94 between St. Paul and Minneapolis were being chosen. The original plan called for freeway access and egress at Prior Avenue. A few blocks south of the freeway on Prior sits St. Mark's Catholic Church and School, one of the leading parishes in the city's dominant religious denomination. That parish was headed for many years by Monsignor Francis J. Gilligan, "the union priest." He was a champion of working people and a national leader of Catholic social justice efforts. A number of politically savvy people were members of that parish, including Doug Kelm, the son of the founding chairman of the merged Democratic-Farmer-Labor Party. With help from allies like Kelm— a future head of the Metropolitan Transit Commission—Father Gilligan asked the state Department of Transportation to put the freeway ramps somewhere else. Putting more traffic on Prior Avenue would be unsafe for schoolchildren and disruptive to church activities, he argued. Somehow, I got peripherally involved and helped get the Prior Avenue ramps eliminated in favor of the Cretin/Vandalia Avenue ramps that are heavily used today.

Monsignor Gilligan had a good memory, his parishioners told me. He was a thrifty sort who kept the church chilly during winter days. But when Jo Anne and Patrick were married on New Year's

Eve day, he turned up the heat in the sanctuary. From him, that was a major gesture of gratitude, I was told.

Jo Anne joined Pat in North Carolina soon after the wedding. Their time together as husband and wife was very brief. On April 1, 1967, his unit was deployed to Vietnam. Jo Anne went next to New York, then came home to Minnesota. Over the next ten months Pat flew over 150 combat missions in an A6, earning many decorations, including two Distinguished Flying Crosses and fourteen air medals. By all accounts he was the best-liked guy in his squadron. He loved to fly, displayed boundless energy, and was willing to assume more than his share of responsibility, his fellow Marines said.

Then that awful lightning struck. Pat's plane failed to return from a mission northwest of Hanoi on January 19, 1968.

Jo Anne was living with us but was not yet home on the day when grim-faced Marines knocked on the door bearing bad news. She arrived shortly after they did and of course exploded in worry and grief. Arlene was so good with her. She knew better than anyone else what Jo was going through.

Like Don Garniss, Pat was "missing in action." But unlike Don, Pat Murray's status would not change in a year or two or three. North Vietnam's reporting of prisoners was very erratic. They initially treated their captives as war criminals and did not adhere to Geneva Convention principles about reporting prisoners taken or treating them with decency. Under those circumstances, the U.S. military was hesitant to change a soldier's status from missing in action (MIA) to killed. Not until all U.S. prisoners of war had been repatriated in 1973 would the Marines say officially that Major Murray had been killed in action. (He was promoted from first lieutenant to captain, then major, while his status was MIA.)

Those years of doubt and uncertainty were awful for Jo Anne and the Murrays, and they were plenty hard on the rest of the family. The Marines asked us not to talk with people outside the family about Pat's MIA status. Their concern was that any public information about who was missing and might be a prisoner would get back to the North Vietnamese and could be used against the U.S. prisoners. They had good evidence that the North Vietnamese were using cruel tactics. We honored the request to keep quiet for much of 1968, as antiwar sentiment swelled in the country and divided Minnesota into camps of doves and hawks. As the home state of both Vice President Hubert Humphrey, who defended U.S. policies until very late in his own unsuccessful bid for the presidency, and Sen. Eugene McCarthy, a prominent critic of those same policies, Minnesota was fixated on Vietnam that year.

Late in the year the *Minneapolis Tribune* published an editorial deploring the fact that Viet Cong captured by the South Vietnamese government were being held in "tiger cages." I was moved to write a letter to the editor in response, saying yes, that's bad, but it's also bad the way American prisoners are being treated by the North Vietnamese. I indicated in the letter that a member of our family was thought to be in that predicament.

That letter served as a rallying cry to other Minnesota families whose soldiers were MIA. In a short while, we came together to form the Minnesota chapter of the National League of Families of Prisoners of War and Missing in Action in Southeast Asia. With so many Americans speaking out in an effort to end the war, I thought it was time for us to become active in the cause of getting U.S. prisoners of war home. I was determined to do everything I could to gain information about Pat's status.

Mary Winn, whose husband David had been a prisoner since August 1968, became our local chapter head. Karlene Everson was involved; her husband Dave was a prisoner for seven or eight years. (Sadly, she died soon after he returned. Dave got into computer work and eventually worked at The St. Paul Companies.) Another active member was Sharon Walsh, whose husband Lt. Col. Richard Walsh was in a plane that went down in flames and was never seen again. His supervisor ruled him MIA. (Sharon was the daughter of Thomas Gallagher, who had run for governor as a Democrat against Harold Stassen in 1938 and went on to twenty-four years of service on the Minnesota Supreme Court. Among the young lawyers who got their start as law clerks to Gallagher was future Vice President Walter Mondale.)

Our POW/MIA group sought speaking opportunities, joining the nation's swelling debate about the war. What an experience! It was demanding, difficult work at a frustrating time. Our message differed from the antiwar movement that was in full force by 1969 and 1970. Many in that movement believed the United States should pull out of Vietnam immediately and unconditionally, and if that meant leaving U.S. prisoners behind, so be it. "We've got to do whatever it takes to get out," I was often told.

Once someone said, "Don't take it personally, but your son-in-law got what was coming to him for America being there." My response: "When you go into the service, nobody can assure you of your safety. That's a risk you take. But if you have the misfortune of getting captured, there's an unwritten contract that your country will never resolve the terms of the conflict without providing for the repatriation of prisoners. You won't be left behind. If that were to happen now, a grave injustice would be committed."

Peace talks had begun in Paris in late 1968, although they were more pretense than negotiations. Months were wasted in a dispute over the shape of the table at which the parties would sit. The real talks that would lead to peace started in late 1969 between Secretary of State Henry Kissinger and Vietnamese Communist Party leader Le Duc Tho. But those exchanges were secret. As far as we Americans knew in 1969, the Paris peace talks were the one available chance for a negotiated settlement that would bring U.S. prisoners home. By then, there were an estimated 1,400 Americans missing or held captive. Our group decided to see what could be done to influence the Paris talks and get any information we could about our missing loved ones. Two small all-female delegations went to Paris with no discernible result. It was decided to try again with a man—me—in the group.

That's how I wound up in Paris in the first week of October 1969 as part of a six-member delegation from the National League of Families of American Prisoners. The U.S. State and Defense departments made the decision that we should go—but we were not to disclose that the government sent us. Our directive was handed down rather abruptly. It was September, and Arlene and I and our dear friends, Margaret and Bill Hruza of Madelia, were taking a few days off in northern Minnesota when Jo Anne was notified that the State Department was trying to reach me. Unbeknownst to her, the four of us had decided to take a day trip to Winnipeg. Jo Anne was desperate to find us and enlisted the help of the sheriff in the county where we had been staying. When we got back to our lake place, there was a note from the sheriff on our door indicating that I was to call him immediately for an urgent message from the State Department. I've often wondered what the sheriff thought.

I was forty-eight years old and had never been overseas except during my military service. My first task was to arrange a leave of absence from The St. Paul Companies and then to get a passport. I discovered that when the State Department wants someone to travel abroad, a passport can be obtained with amazing speed.

I flew to Long Island to meet with the other members of our delegation, whom I had not met before. I was to present myself as the women's male escort, chosen by them—though the choosing had in fact been done by the U.S. Departments of State and Defense. Among the five women in our group was our organization's founder and national president, Sybil Stockdale from Coronado, California. Her husband, James Stockdale, was the highest-ranking officer imprisoned in North Vietnam. He eventually retired as a vice admiral. He gained national notice in 1992 as Texas businessman H. Ross Perot's running mate in a third-party bid for the presidency.

Another delegation member was Pat Mearns, whose husband Arthur was an Air Force major and had been missing for three years at that point. *Life* magazine was following Pat for a feature story that was published on November 7, 1969, and included a photo of our group walking and talking on a Paris street. Arthur Mearns was promoted to colonel before he was confirmed to have died; his remains came home in 1977. The others in our group were Ruth Ann Parisho and Candy Parish, both married to missing Navy lieutenants and living in Virginia Beach, Virginia, and Andrea Rander, whose husband S.Sgt. Donald Rander was a known prisoner of the Viet Cong. Of our group of six, only two knew with certainty that their loved ones were prisoners. Only those two would come home again.

After a few days of briefings, we flew to Paris and found rooms in the Inter-Continental Hotel. The women roomed together; I had a separate room. We were to make an effort to see the North Vietnamese delegation then resident in Choisy-le-Roi, a commune in a suburban area southeast of Paris, and Madame Nguyen Thi Binh, a leading delegate from the communist insurgent front that Americans called the Viet Cong. We conveyed our request for a meeting and waited. And waited. We did not dare all leave the hotel at once for fear that we would miss a call.

We were more or less on our own. The U.S. government had arranged for us to go, but there could be no sign of a government connection after we arrived. The government wasn't picking up the tab. I had a little money with me, but the rest of the group began to worry about the cost of our stay. A full week passed. Then the call came. We could meet the North Vietnamese delegation for tea at their Choisy-le-Roi headquarters.

The meeting was not unpleasant. We were ushered into an ordinary room in a former school building. We came bearing modest gifts of cigarettes; they gave us candy and served tea and sweets. Sybil took the lead; I backed her up. We presented ourselves as individual American citizens worried about our loved ones whom we believed might be captives in their country. We asked for information about our 1,400 missing servicemen and for release of those held as prisoners. At one point, Sybil wanted to read a statement she had prepared, but she discovered she had forgotten her reading glasses. One of the North Vietnamese handed her his own glasses so that she could proceed. I took that simple act of kindness as a positive sign.

But the Vietnamese had no response to our pleas. At one point, they seemed annoyed, saying that visits by Americans were unnecessary. If we wanted to do something for peace, we should join antiwar groups at home, they said. They made the point that while several hundred Americans were deemed missing in action, many times more of their countrymen were missing—which was the truth. They showed us a propaganda film. They offered bland, general assurances that if our men were prisoners, they were well cared for. But in fact, Jim Stockdale was enduring repeated beatings. When he was finally released in February 1973, his shoulders had been wrenched from their sockets, his leg was shattered, and his back was broken.

Madame Binh refused to see us, but our request may have made some impression on her about the extent of concern Americans felt about the POWs. In 1971 she advanced a peace proposal that essentially offered a trade: if the United States would set a date for withdrawal, the American POWs could come home.

News reporters were waiting for us when we left the North Vietnamese and again when I got home to St. Paul. I tried not to sound too discouraged, fearing that doing so would harm our cause. It was hard to see any discernible progress then, but I believe now that it served the POWs well for their captors to see that an organized force had developed to advocate on the prisoners' behalf. We learned eventually that treatment of the prisoners improved at about the time we got organized. Solitary confinements and beatings diminished. I like to think that happened because the North Vietnamese understood that they would ultimately be held accountable for the welfare of the Americans they held captive.

It wasn't easy for Jo Anne and all of us to watch the U.S. prisoners come home in 1973 and see that Pat was not among them. His status changed to "killed in action" in 1974, but some doubt lingered in all of our minds. Patrick was the love of her life. She didn't want to let him go. She took a job as a substitute teacher in St. Paul not long after learning of his disappearance. Soon thereafter she became a full-time teacher in St. Paul, specializing in English language learning. In 1989 she married Ed Driscoll, an attorney with the Larkin Hoffman firm.

In late 1986—almost nineteen years after Pat's plane went down—we got word from the Marine Corps that his remains had been identified. It was a bittersweet time, bringing both renewed sorrow and welcome closure. The North Vietnamese had repatriated a large box of skeletal remains that included part of Patrick's jaw and arm. His severed body had been buried along with that of other missing U.S. aviators not long after his plane was felled by a surface-to-air missile, we later learned.

We had a funeral for Pat on December 22, 1986, at the chapel at the University of St. Thomas, and those incomplete remains were buried at Fort Snelling Cemetery. Some years later, using DNA evidence, more of his remains were identified. Some of those remains were added to the Fort Snelling site; others, found close to the remains of the pilot of Patrick's plane, Major Hobart Wallace, were buried under a headstone bearing both of their names at Arlington National Cemetery. Both additional burials occasioned another sad ceremony. For so long, we didn't know where Patrick was. In the end, he was buried three times.

I spoke at the December 22, 1986, funeral and conveyed some of the mixed feelings that the Vietnam War stirred in nearly everyone it touched: "Pat Murray, a real patriot who loved his country and was anxious to come home, put his life on the line for his country in a cause many of us today still struggle to comprehend. He lost, and in so doing, we all lost because it is clear he truly had the right stuff, the talent to make our communities better places to live. Pat lost his life in what may seem to have been such a waste. Clearly, we must find better ways of avoiding war and preserving peace. But we still need men and women willing under some circumstances to take risks, ready to make sacrifices for whatever the cause, including that of their country.

"Pat's ultimate sacrifice would be a waste only if those of us who loved him and survive forget him, what he was, what he did, and why."

POSTSCRIPT: Our MIA families' organization's head, Sybil Stockdale, is a widow now, ailing with Parkinson's disease. I remain in contact with her, even though she cannot speak. Her aide tells me that my calls are a comfort to her. The Stockdales had four sons, all of whom went into education. One of them was for a time dean of students at Blake School in the Twin Cities.

I followed James Stockdale's career after he came home. He won the Congressional Medal of Honor for his leadership at the Hanoi Hilton, under extraordinarily trying conditions. In 1979, he became superintendent of the Citadel, a military school in South Carolina, and tried to rein in that school's notorious culture of discipline and hazing. He resigned after one year when the board of trustees refused to back his efforts. I admired that stance. He ended his career teaching Greek history at Stanford University.

During the war I was a defender of American policy in Vietnam. After Patrick was lost, I would have felt somehow disloyal to him if I'd voiced doubts about the American mission in Vietnam. But doubts arose later. I learned at one point that Jim Stockdale—who had been a squadron commander on an aircraft carrier in August 1964—said that the Gulf of Tonkin incident "never happened." Americans had been told that the North Vietnamese had instigated a hostile exchange with an American vessel. President Lyndon Johnson used the Tonkin incident to justify a U.S. military buildup. Subsequent historical accounts say that one incident did occur on August 2, but it was instigated by the U.S. ship, not the North Vietnamese. Johnson told Americans about a second incident at sea two days later that was never confirmed. I'd like to think that this country wouldn't go to war again on such shaky premises. But as Americans saw during the run-up to the war in Iraq in 2003—and as our family knows too well—history is prone to repeating itself.

CHAPTER 21

DARE

I N AUGUST 1968, as our family worried about Jo Anne's husband
Patrick, lost over North Vietnam, Americans watched with dismay as protests outside the Democratic National Convention in Chicago devolved into mayhem and violence. A subsequent fact-finding commission termed the episode "a police riot." Mayor Richard Daley gave orders for the police to crack down hard on those who came to Chicago to object to U.S. involvement in Vietnam. The result was a national embarrassment that likely contributed to Hubert Humphrey's defeat in that year's presidential election. By unfair extension, it also eroded Americans' respect for their own local police forces. They were routinely termed "pigs"—and that was among the kinder things said.

I was active in the St. Paul Chamber of Commerce, and I went to its executive director Amos Martin that fall with an idea. St. Paul should take pride in the professionalism and fairness of its police force, I noted. Wouldn't this be a good time for the chamber to show our appreciation? They agreed, and we formed a police relations committee, officially the Chamber Committee on Public Conduct and Concern. I would be its chair for the next twenty or so years, working with police chiefs Lester McAuliffe, Richard Rowan, and Bill McCutcheon.

We made clear to the police department that we intended to support their mission, but we were not intending to be knee-jerk defenders. We would raise money for special projects, inform ourselves about the issues they faced, and speak publicly on their behalf when we deemed them unfairly criticized. In exchange, we would share our ideas and expect a respectful hearing.

Our projects were varied. We raised money for bullet-resistant glass for all squad cars. We supplied bulletproof vests for all the officers. We provided the funds to enable undercover police to buy drugs from pushers or to buy information from informants when that was warranted. The *Pioneer Press* became interested and dispatched an investigative reporter to determine whether we were doing something improper. The reporter couldn't come up with a story.

One of our committee's members was the president of Minnesota Mutual Life Insurance, Harold Cummings, a great guy and a real asset to our effort. Harold, then in his sixties, often rode with us on the "police power squad"—the 8:00 P.M. to 4:00 A.M. shift. One committee member would ride with one officer to learn more about our city at nighttime. Not many CEOs would exhibit that much concern for his firm's hometown.

When I went on "power squad" rides, I concluded that police work was not my calling. If I had been a policeman, World War III would have started. Patience is a quality that is critical to police work, and the officers whose work I witnessed possessed much more patience than I would have had, had I been in their shoes.

They were also highly observant. One of my first nights riding with an officer was in late November. We were driving on Lexington Avenue near Central High School. A car passed us, and without saying a word to me, the officer turned on his siren and signal lights and pulled the car over. That driver had done nothing wrong that I could detect. I jumped to a too-hasty conclusion that the officer was too eager. I stayed in the squad car as the officer left to speak to the driver. When the officer returned to the squad car, I asked about the stop in a tone that betrayed my suspicion. The officer calmly informed me that he had noticed that the car's muffler was loose. He stopped the young driver simply to inform him of that fact and urge him to get it repaired soon.

"Tom, those are young people, and they've got a bad muffler," he said. "It's getting cold out. Young people tend to spoon in their cars, and they leave the engine running when it's cold. A bad muffler could lead to carbon monoxide getting into the car and real trouble for those kids." I felt sheepish—and pleased that someone so observant and thoughtful was serving our city.

Positive relationships developed through the chamber committee that were a plus for the whole community. They were noticed beyond St. Paul. In April 1971 I was invited to address the annual meeting of the U.S. Chamber of Commerce in Washington, DC, to report about our work. "Every man on the force knows the business community is concerned about his work and welfare and isn't sitting idly on the sidelines. . . . When the chief or the commissioner of public safety needs help, he knows where to come with the assurance that he'll get it. Conversely, when the business community is concerned about specific or broad problems involving police matters, it receives prompt and accurate information." I added that St. Paul's crime rate was down 5.4 percent in 1970 over 1969—a rare achievement among large American cities that year.

In late 1988 or early 1989, Police Chief Bill McCutcheon came to our committee with a suggestion. In Los Angeles, a partnership between police and the business community had produced a program in that city's schools that appeared to be effective in deterring drug abuse by young people. It had the ancillary benefit of creating positive relationships between youngsters and police officers, generating more respect for police work generally. Los Angeles had been using the program since 1983, and cities in forty-six other states were in the process of adopting similar programs. "I think we should do it," McCutcheon said. We did. That's how DARE came to St. Paul.

DARE was an acronym for Drug Abuse Resistance Education. It entailed taking six officers away from their regular duties and deploying them into all of the city's fifth- and sixth-grade classrooms, public and private, where they would meet with students to discuss the dangers of illicit drugs. This wouldn't be a short course. Seventeen one-hour presentations per class were contemplated, along with curricular materials for student use and training for the officers. Lt. Gary Briggs, an officer with a strong academic background, worked with us to create the program. Its initial budget was $200,000 a year. Our arrangement was that in its first year, 1989–90, our chamber committee would raise 80 percent of its operating funds, with the school district and the police force splitting the remaining 20 percent of the cost. I was the chief fund-raiser and found a major backer in 3M, which donated $100,000 that first year. In subsequent years, as the program proved its value, the business share would drop until the fifth year, when it would be entirely financed by the school district and the police force. It was a classic public–private partnership.

It's hard to measure DARE's success in deterring drug abuse, though we have anecdotal claims that it made a difference in young lives. But there's abundant testimony about DARE changing kids' attitudes about cops. Teachers who are generally cool to opening their classrooms to outside programming came to welcome DARE. The police officers took their teaching role seriously and worked hard at connecting with at-risk kids. They stayed at the schools during lunch and recess to build friendships. My grandchildren told me they truly enjoyed the officer-led classes. Rather than disrespecting police, students came to admire them. The law enforcement community evidently saw its value too. In 1993 I was presented with the FBI Director's Community Leadership Award for my work establishing DARE.

DARE ended when a budget crunch came. Its inability to quantify long-term success made it vulnerable when public money became tight. Yet I have no doubt that DARE had lasting impact. Insistence on funding only those efforts whose results can be quantified can cause us to underappreciate some things of real value.

CHAPTER 22

"Don't Leave Home without It"

IN THE EARLY 1980S, St. Paul Fire and Marine owned Western Life Insurance. I was invited to address a national sales meeting of Western agents at a southern Colorado resort. That seemed like a fine excuse for Arlene and me to take a few days and explore a part of the country we did not know well. Before the meeting, we headed to Santa Fe, New Mexico.

On our last night there, our hotel concierge recommended a small Hispanic-owned restaurant in a converted monastery. Off we went. We were seated in a room with only four tables, each of them occupied. Nearest to us were three men, one of whom became louder and coarser as the evening progressed. When the waiter brought that table their check, that fellow presented his American Express card as payment. "I'm sorry, sir, but we don't accept American Express," the waiter said. What ensued was the foulest dialogue of vitriol and complaint I had ever heard in a restaurant. The waiter went to get the restaurant manager. The two others with the man with the American Express card offered to pay the bill with cash. "No! This is a matter of principle!" the loudmouth replied.

The proprietor arrived, and the abuse continued. "American Express is legal tender!" the cardholder said. That was news to me. The proprietor said, "I'm going to have to call the police." "Call 'em!" the offensive patron said. The call was made. Soon police officers arrived and took the three men away. Arlene and I sat slack-jawed, taking in this entire spectacle.

When it was time for us to pay our check, I felt I needed to say something. "I apologize for the way that fellow acted," I said.

"I ought to apologize to you!" the proprietor said. I wondered aloud what would happen to the three fellows in police custody. "I don't know, and I don't care," he said. Arlene and I marveled all the way back to the hotel at the extreme attachment some Americans have to their credit cards.

Another credit card episode made the next day of our trip memorable, too. We were in Taos, New Mexico, the location of a centuries-old pueblo community. We toured it, then visited a pueblo curio shop. A Navajo shopkeeper wearing a GI-issued T-shirt greeted us. Arlene found some Zuni jewelry she admired and a belt buckle for me. The shopkeeper asked her to guess the price. She named a price she considered fair, and he replied that her bid was high. He named a lower price, allowing that the overhead costs at a shop with a dirt floor were modest. The sign said, "Credit cards welcome," so I whipped mine out.

"Gee, I'll have to call this in," the shopkeeper said.

"OK," I said.

"But I don't have a phone here," he continued. "I have to go to my sister's house to make the call. Usually my wife is here to watch the shop while I go, but she's not here now." He was alone in the shop.

I didn't have enough cash to make the purchase, and I thought that this fellow needed this sale. So I made an offer: "You go make the call, and I'll stay here and mind your store for you. I can handle postcard and greeting card sales, and if a prospective buyer of jewelry shows up, I'll try to hold him or her here until you return."

He must have decided I was trustworthy. He agreed, and I moved behind the counter. But just as the shopkeeper was about to leave, his wife came in. He briefed her on the situation.

"Do you have a personal check?" she asked.

Yes, I said, but it's from Minnesota.

She thought for a second. "That'll do," she said. She evidently figured that if her husband had decided I was fit to mind the store, I was probably good for the check. We left with our purchases and with a twinge of regret. I never again would have the opportunity to become the interim proprietor of a curio shop in the most authentic pueblo in North America.

CHAPTER 23

Insurance Encore

As a Republican, I didn't have a close relationship with DFL Gov. Rudy Perpich. But since he was governor for ten years—longer than any other Minnesotan—most Minnesotans who were active in public affairs had some familiarity with him. I didn't realize how close he considered our acquaintance until I had an unexpected call at the office one day.

"Hi, it's Rudy," the caller said.

It took me a beat or two to realize that this was the governor calling and to respond appropriately.

It was 1989, and Perpich's longtime commerce commissioner, Mike Hatch, was resigning from that post. His intention, which became clear soon thereafter, was to run against Rudy in the 1990 DFL gubernatorial primary. He did and lost.

Minnesota's commerce commissioner's responsibilities include insurance regulation. Hatch, a feisty attorney who later became state's attorney general, was not viewed as receptive to insurance industry input. The industry's local leaders had let Perpich know that they hoped Hatch's successor would be more open to their concerns. Someone close to Perpich had already contacted me and inquired about my interest in succeeding Hatch. I pooh-poohed the suggestion, pointing out that my politics were wrong for the Perpich administration.

"Your name has been mentioned" for commerce commissioner, Perpich said to me on the phone. I noticed that he didn't say, "I want you for the job." I reiterated what I'd said to his go-between earlier—that as a known Republican, I wasn't well suited to a prominent role in his cabinet. He accepted that and then said, "Have you got a recommendation for me?" He mentioned a few names. I knew one—Minneapolis attorney Tom Borman—and shared my positive impression of him.

A few days later, quite early in the morning, I had another call: "Hi, it's Rudy." He was calling to tell me that he would announce Borman's appointment at a news conference later that day. That call was a courtesy that I had not expected but appreciated.

The biggest Minnesota insurance issue in those years was the high cost of workers' compensation insurance borne by employers. Workers' comp relief had topped the state Chamber of Commerce's wish list at every legislative session since the late 1970s. Those costs were high due to a combination of legislative action, case law, and regulatory decisions by the state's insurance commissioner, who reported to the commissioner of commerce. The DFL politicians who controlled state government through most of the 1980s were loath to shrink benefits for injured workers in response to employers' pleas for relief. But in 1983, the Legislature tried another cost-control tactic—competition. It created the State Fund Mutual Insurance Co., a member-owned mutual workers' compensation company, to compete with private insurers. Today, that firm's name is SFM, "The Work Comp Experts."

State Fund Mutual did not fully satisfy employers, who were still clamoring for legislative changes in workers' comp law as the Perpich administration ended in January 1991, but its rates were low enough to make it a commercial success. By 1991 it was the state's largest provider of workers' comp insurance, serving 5,500 employers.

That year, Republican Arne Carlson succeeded Perpich as governor, Bert McKasy succeeded Borman as commerce commissioner, and the economy tumbled into a recession just deep enough to reveal that State Fund Mutual's investment practices had been too risky. The firm was in trouble. McKasy came to me to ask whether I'd be willing to be State Fund Mutual's interim CEO and help correct the problem.

I turned seventy years old in 1991. I figured that I still had something in the tank. I accepted—perhaps a bit too quickly. I didn't bother to find out where State Fund Mutual's headquarters were located. I simply assumed that because it had been created by state government, it was in St. Paul. I discovered to my chagrin that my new office was in Eden Prairie, a southwest metro suburb. I was not only back at a full-time job but had acquired a miserably long commute. Patience behind the wheel of a car has never been my strong suit.

McKasy worked with me to devise a financial rescue plan. It involved a loan from another state-created workers' compensation entity, the Workers Compensation Reinsurance Association, to help us with cash flow. Three members of the reinsurance association's board joined our board as a condition of that loan. With the help of a quick economic recovery, we climbed out of our financial hole. I shifted soon thereafter from interim CEO to chair of the State Fund Mutual governing board, a position I held until 1996.

CHAPTER 24

Health Reformer

DISTRESS WAS RISING IN 1992 over the cost and quality of the nation's health care system, and characteristically, Minnesota was ahead of other states in trying to solve the problem. Collaboration between DFL Sen. Linda Berglin and Republican Sen. Duane Benson in the 1992 Legislature led to the creation of a state-subsidized insurance program for the working poor, MinnesotaCare. Their bill also established a twenty-six-member Minnesota Health Care Commission and gave it a daunting assignment: recommend a strategy for reforming the practice of medicine in order to put the brakes on rising costs. Its goal was a seemingly modest 10 percent per year reduction in the rate of health care cost increases in each of the five years beginning in 1995. The push for cost containment was a bow to employers, who were not happy that MinnesotaCare would be financed by a tax on health care bills that they would ultimately pay. If they were going to be hit with a state "provider tax"—which some called the "sick tax"—they at least wanted the state to do what it could to squeeze health care costs.

Gov. Arne Carlson chose me to fill the commission seat reserved for a consumer who was past age sixty-five. At the advice of his chief of staff Curt Johnson, my old Citizens League ally, he also tapped me as commission chair. When the governor called to recruit me, I asked him how much time he expected the work to consume. "About three months," he said. It was the start of three years of very full-time volunteer work leading to the production of six major reports.

My initial interest in the commission's work centered on cost containment. But I soon came to see that the inability of low-income working people to affordably obtain insurance was an economic and social disgrace. I wanted to do something to solve that problem too.

The commission was loaded with expertise. It included leaders of the state's health care industry as well as representatives of business and labor and a few current and future state agency heads. My challenge as chair wasn't going to be to bring these people up to speed—many of them knew the issue better than I did. The challenge was to gain consensus, given their disparate perspectives. Dr. Jasper Daube, the Mayo Clinic department of neurology head who was one of two representatives of the Minnesota Medical Association on the commission, asked me at the outset whether I intended to employ Robert's Rules of Order in our meetings.

"I haven't thought about that, but I guess we will," I said somewhat vaguely. What I didn't say aloud was that while I favor orderly meetings, I didn't want to be hamstrung by procedure. What mattered most was achieving as much consensus as possible. Some meetings later, when achieving that goal meant ruling the voluble Dr. Daube out of order—even though under Robert's Rules he had the floor—I ruled that he be silent. That evidently was noticed. When my service on the commission ended, *St. Paul Pioneer Press* editorial writer Steve Dornfeld quoted Curt Johnson: "When (Swain) had to divert from Robert's venerable rules, he did it. He got people who weren't accustomed to being in the same room to agree."

We had the good fortune to hire the superb Michael Scandrett as our executive director. He worked exceedingly hard. He understood my desire to achieve consensus among commission members on whatever we proposed. With not much fanfare and a tight deadline for the first of our reports, we set out to show the nation what a progressive state could do to offer better health care at a more affordable price. Our first recommendations were to be delivered to the 1993 Legislature; we started meeting in earnest in August 1992.

That first report attacked the major issue—cost containment—head-on. It recommended an approach that, under changed names and acronyms, is at the heart of today's national health care reform efforts. The notion was to switch the health care reimbursement system to reward value, not volume. We may have been the first to call for the formation of integrated service networks: groups of physicians, clinics, hospitals, and associated health care providers that contracted with purchasers of health insurance to provide a full range of services at a fixed cost to a given population. Today's accountable care organizations are based on the same concept.

The idea was to provide incentives for health providers to keep people healthy, which costs a great deal less than treating them after they are ill. Instead of paying for every medical procedure that is performed, which creates an incentive for more and more procedures, integrated service networks (ISNs) would be paid on a per-person, per-year basis. Keeping covered people healthy would allow any unspent yearly compensation to go to the network's bottom line. We proposed that the state health commissioner set an annual limit on the rate of growth in health care spending for each ISN. Health care providers would not be required to participate in ISNs under our scheme, but if ISNs worked as intended, doctors and hospitals would find good financial reason to participate.

We worked hard to get unanimous support from the commission for our first report. The sentiment was quite enthusiastic except for some skepticism among representatives of my own insurance industry. But legislators, particularly Republicans, took aim at the first report's comments about the need for health care consumers to do their part in reducing costs and for government to give them more reasons to do the right thing. We called for an increase in tobacco and cigarette taxes, enactment of a law requiring seat belt use in vehicles and helmets by cyclists and recreational vehicle operators, and more health support for pregnant women. We elaborated on those ideas in a major report in February 1994.

To me, those ideas were among the most important ones we advanced. A large portion of the increase in health care costs can be attributed to Americans not taking care of themselves as they should. The commission's 1993 proposal was for a 23-cent per-pack increase in cigarette taxes. I would have gone further. I favored a gradual, sustained increase in the cigarette tax, 20 cents per year over a period of ten years. The proceeds of that increase could be dedicated to providing health insurance for the low-income uninsured. It was a win-win idea. Studies found that for every 10 percent increase in the cost of a package of cigarettes, consumption would fall 4 percent among the population as a whole and nearly 20 percent among teenagers. We could give more people the benefits of health insurance while driving down smoking rates, thereby improving overall public health.

The idea fell flat at the time, even though Minnesota's per-pack cigarette tax in the 1990s was a modest 48 cents. Flanked by Senators Berglin and Benson, I testified in favor of a tobacco tax increase before the Senate Tax Committee. We got it past that first procedural hurdle. But then the tobacco industry hired every lobbyist left standing in the state. They raised the specter of large numbers of Minnesota smokers driving across state lines to buy cigarettes and other sundries to the detriment of this state's retailers and sales tax receipts. We argued that some state ought to take the lead in deterring smoking, and if Minnesota played that role, adjoining states would follow suit. I still think that argument has merit, but at that time, it wouldn't sell.

We learned later that in other states, particularly California, the tobacco industry's main objection wasn't to the higher tax; it was for the use of the new tax to finance antismoking educational efforts among teenagers. The industry was afraid those deterrence programs would work, and for good reason—they did.

Not until a money crisis in state government and a partial government shutdown in 2005 did the cigarette tax climb by 75 cents per pack, and then only after DFLers agreed to Republican Gov. Tim Pawlenty's insistence that it be called a "health impact fee." The breakthrough finally came in 2013 under a DFL Legislature and DFL governor, when a $1.60-per-pack tax was added. That brings Minnesota's total per-pack tax to $2.83—the highest in the Upper Midwest but still modest compared with New York ($4.35) and most New England states.

The resistance was nearly as strong when we pushed for a requirement that motorcyclists wear helmets while driving. We took our 1993 commission meetings on the road to expose more of the state to our work. One of those meetings was at Mayo Clinic in Rochester, at an auditorium in their complex. When I arrived on the stage, the auditorium's first rows of seats were already full with people who, judging from their garb, had all arrived via motorcycle. They were a burly group, intent on delivering one message simply by their presence: don't mess with us.

One of my thrills in connection with the commission was an invitation to address the medical staff of the Mayo Clinic at one of their regular meetings. These are among the best physicians in the world. I was invited to appear on March 8, 1995, to provide an update on our commission's work. I allowed that I "feel somewhat like the proverbial fellow bringing coals to Newcastle." But I soldiered on with a talk touting the benefits of MinnesotaCare and the commission's early reform work. Growth in the share of the state's population without health insurance had stopped with the advent of low-cost, subsidized health insurance for the working poor, I reported. Some 78,000 more Minnesotans had insurance in 1995 than in 1992. Welfare caseloads were down as low-income Minnesotans found it possible to obtain health care coverage without leaving the workforce. A new state purchasing pool was helping more employers affordably offer health insurance benefits to their employees. Insurance cost increases had slowed. More quality measures were being made and were on their way to health care consumers.

I also acknowledged the challenge of achieving the goal that the 1994 Legislature set for us—universal coverage. We knew quite a bit by 1995 about who lacked insurance. Fully one-third of them were people with incomes exceeding 275 percent of the federal poverty guidelines. Those were people we thought could afford insurance, but they weren't buying. Disproportionately, they were single men between the ages of eighteen and thirty-four. "The size of this voluntarily uninsured group is much larger than anticipated. It was the big surprise of this research," I told the Mayo audience. "Unless most of this group decides to pay its way and become insured, it will not be possible to achieve universal coverage."

That population is now a focus of national health care reform efforts. The Affordable Care Act (ACA)—"Obamacare"—attempts to compel those people to buy insurance and, for those with low incomes, to make it affordable. But even though the U.S. Supreme Court ruled that requirement constitutional, it has met with enormous resistance, particularly among Republicans with a libertarian bent. Already in 1994, our commission was calling for a "freeloader penalty" of $500 per voluntarily uninsured person in the first year and more each year thereafter. We recognized then what the ACA acknowledges: keeping health insurance affordable for all requires the purchase of insurance by all.

As I told the Mayo audience in 1995, the uninsured did not lack for medical treatment. They could go to a hospital emergency room at any time and did, often at needlessly high cost. When they could not pay that cost themselves, it was passed along to the insured population via higher premiums. Uncompensated care was already costing Minnesotans $213 million in 1994. Eighteen years later—shortly before the advent of the ACA—that cost had swelled to $521 million. I believe that without a coverage mandate and a freeloader penalty to back it up, that figure would soon have swelled to more than $1 billion per year. That's a hidden tax burden. It's one of the reasons that employers are increasingly eager to drop health insurance benefits for their employees. That's what is coming if the ACA isn't able to push the freeloaders into the health insurance pool.

In Minnesota in 1993 and 1994, our commission came up with ideas that could have brought the basic structure of the ACA to this state almost twenty years before it arrived in the rest of the country. What's more, our operation was a classic example of a public–private partnership that produced a lot of consensus while operating in full public view. But by 1995, insurance cost increases were leveling off, and the political will to do something dramatic for the sake of better, more affordable health care was waning. The commission was ready for a major push for universal coverage in 1995, but Governor Carlson and the Legislature were not. They repealed the move to integrated service networks that they had supported two years earlier. Similarly, in Washington, the health reform effort led by First Lady Hillary Clinton faltered in Congress amid heavy opposition from the insurance industry. With some frustration, I submitted my resignation from the Minnesota Health Care Commission in August 1995.

The concept we advanced—paying for outcomes rather than for volume—still strikes me as promising. We'll be a better society if we can compensate the medical profession for keeping people healthy by preventing chronic conditions like diabetes, heart disease, lung cancer, and eventually Alzheimer's disease. We'll be better if we can give everyone the preventive care that keeps people out of high-cost emergency rooms. The ACA is a start toward moving in that direction. If the ACA approach fails, I predict reformers will be pushing harder for something I wasn't ready to support in 1994—Medicare for all, a single-payer system. If I'm still around, I might push with them. American health care before the ACA was a social, economic, and moral disgrace. We can't go back.

CHAPTER 25

Gopher Tales

IN 1976, I became the national president of the University of Minnesota Alumni Association. That organization's executive director since 1948 was Ed Haislet, a former boxing coach with a punchy personality to match. He would tell university presidents that he reported to our association's executive committee, and he would tell the committee that he reported to the president. In his mind, he was a free agent, operating with one strong notion: alumni were to be served by the institution. They were to be regarded as great friends whose needs and wishes were to be accommodated. In Haislet's view, the university should not risk alienating these allies by asking them for financial contributions.

That was the attitude C. Peter Magrath found in the alumni office when he became president in late 1974. It didn't match his thinking—nor that of probably any other university alumni office in the country. He told me and my predecessor as association president, Wally Salovich, "You tell Haislet that he's through."

Magrath likely didn't know that he was giving us a potentially daunting assignment. Haislet had a reputation for a strong temper and a willingness to resolve disputes by saying, "Let's go outside and settle this like men." That was his modus operandi even when he was past age seventy. I'd seen as much a few years earlier when, as association vice president, I oversaw the development of the association's Alumni Club at the top of the IDS Building in downtown Minneapolis. Haislet gave the construction people on the project such a hard time that they complained to me, "He's going to give us heart attacks!" When I took up the issue with him, he said, "If they can't deal with me, they ought to have heart attacks."

Salovich and I met with Haislet in a private room at the St. Paul Athletic Club. I did so with trepidation, fearing that he might create a scene. As decently as we could, we told him that it was time for him to retire. I can't say that he accepted the news graciously. But he didn't physically challenge us either, so I considered the meeting a success. We remained on good terms.

While I was president, I changed the Alumni Association's message. "It's time for us to recognize that we received a highly subsidized education," I'd say in speeches to various college constituencies. Taxes and donations paid a significant portion of our educational costs, "and we owe the same thing to those who follow." Alumni giving at the University of Minnesota ranked dead last in the Big Ten when Haislet left. Today it's in the middle of the pack.

WHEN ALUMNI ASSOCIATION PRESIDENT Penny Winton, who served in 1985–86, called for reform in the way members are elected to the University of Minnesota Board of Regents, she appointed a committee to explore change. There had been grousing about the ease with which people with strong political ties could land on what was probably the most important governing board in the state while more talented leaders without political connections were denied a chance to serve. The state constitution was at the root of that problem; it specified that the Board of Regents would be elected by the most politically minded body in the state, the Legislature.

Winton's committee was a great group, with former governor Elmer Andersen, AFL-CIO leader Neil Sherburne, and Ken Dayton of Dayton-Hudson Corp. among them. I was there too. We came up with the idea that a bipartisan screening panel should be created to recommend candidates to the Legislature. Elmer asked me to be in charge of an implementation strategy. I raised some money and found legislative sponsors—Rep. Todd Otis, the son of Elmer's Supreme Court appointee James Otis, and Sen. Ember Reichgott Junge—to carry the bill enacting the change. But the idea didn't go very far. It was perceived as taking authority away from the Legislature—never an easy sell with legislators—and was opposed by the sitting regents.

Then the Eastcliff scandal hit. President Ken Keller was suddenly under heavy fire for what was perceived as overspending on the remodeling of his official residence, Eastcliff. He was also faulted for a $50 million reserve fund, the existence of which was mysteriously unknown to some regents. And his academic plan, Commitment to Focus, was being faulted in some quarters as elitist. It was a bum rap in my opinion on all counts. He was right on track, but he was alone. The regents choked in the face of pressure. Keller was pushed out of the presidency in March 1988, three years after he had taken office. It was like a public execution.

I was in Florida when I had a phone call from state Sen. Gene Waldorf, the St. Paul DFLer in charge of higher education funding in the Senate. He wanted to revive our committee's proposal for a regents' screening panel. The Legislature had reason to think that the Board of Regents had not been sufficiently attentive to its responsibilities and needed improvement. With only about six weeks remaining in the legislative session, he wanted to move right now. Some businesspeople stepped up to push our case, hiring respected lobbyist Larry Redmond to help. Our plan became law.

The Regent Candidate Advisory Council, a twenty-four-member group with mixed political backgrounds, was operational in time for the 1989 legislative session's election of regents. The founding council was headed by St. Olaf College president Melvin George; I was its first vice chair. Our assignment was to identify and recruit applicants for the twelve-member board and recommend at least two, but no more than four, candidates for each vacant seat. We took the work seriously. Ken Dayton was exceedingly thorough. He told me that he personally called more than two hundred people to check the references of applicants during his years on the council. He and I became good friends.

I'd like to say that the council worked like a charm and that governance at the university is much improved as a result. But nothing is foolproof. There have been mistakes along the way, and the Legislature has still found ways to play politics with regents' selection. I will claim that the overall caliber and commitment of regents has improved in the past twenty-five years, and that would not have happened without the screening the council did every two years.

WHEN PEOPLE LAMENT that business leaders don't get involved as much as they might in public service, I think of David Lilly. He was a marvelous man with a brilliant financial mind, and he cared very much about Minnesota. Lilly headed the Toro Co. for thirty-three years, from 1945 to 1978. During those years he was an active citizen, doing such things as serving as finance chairman for Elmer Andersen's campaign for governor. He retired to serve a brief stint on the Federal Reserve Board of Governors and then became dean of the University of Minnesota's School of Management. He was appointed university-wide vice president for finance and operations, just in time for furor to erupt over Keller and the reserve fund in 1987–88. Lilly was hammered in the news media—unjustifiably so, in my opinion. He stuck it out at the university until 1992, when he retired at age seventy-five. He died in February 2014 at age ninety-six. David was well-known and highly regarded in business circles, and his experience at the university was widely noticed. It illustrates why some business people are hesitant to move into the public arena. This state is the poorer for it.

ABOUT THE TIME I RETIRED from The St. Paul Companies in 1986, Arlene and I attended the gathering of a couples dinner club that had been meeting regularly for many years. We all knew each other well enough to share personal thoughts. Our hostess Ruth Hultgren suggested a topic for the evening: what do you aspire to do in retirement? I had a ready answer: I want to do something in service to the University of Minnesota. I didn't know what that might be, I said, but if my alma mater called, I would respond.

The call came ten years later, at a meeting at Eastcliff. Ed Spencer, a longtime executive at Honeywell, had convened a group of civic leaders with university ties to consider what we might do to help President Nils Hasselmo, who was nearing the end of what had been a difficult presidency. He'd been caught in the middle of a major struggle between a faction on the Board of Regents and the faculty over tenure policy. He was also handicapped by strained relationships with the business community and Gov. Arne Carlson. Those at the table that day agreed that Hasselmo might benefit from bringing a senior adviser into his administration, both to assist him and to reassure disgruntled constituencies. Spencer turned to me and said, "Will you do it?"

I couldn't say no. In July 1996, at age seventy-five, I became the university's interim vice president for institutional relations. My job was to help Hasselmo put a positive coda on his presidency and, in so doing, strengthen the hands of the committee that was about to begin a search for his successor.

I thought I could be helpful in patching up any hard feelings that had developed among the state's employers, but I wasn't sure how to proceed with Carlson. I had put in more than three years of almost full-time volunteer work on health care reform as a Carlson appointee and hardly got his attention. Just as I was coming on board at the university, Carlson was publicly criticizing Hasselmo's demotion the previous year of Dr. John Najarian as chair of the department of surgery at the medical school. Najarian had recently been acquitted on federal tax evasion charges related to the sale and use of an organ transplant drug he had developed. But Carlson interjected himself before the federal investigation of the use of research funds had been completed. It was a tense, awkward situation.

I thought the least I could do was try to find out what had gone wrong between Hasselmo and Carlson. I sought a meeting with Morrie Anderson, Carlson's chief of staff—thinking that as a former occupant of that office, I might at least get the courtesy of an appointment. I didn't get an answer. I called a few times, then decided to contact Anderson's predecessor as chief of staff, Curtis Johnson, for advice. Curt had been the executive director of the Citizens League when I was its president in 1985–86. Johnson went to bat for me and got me an appointment.

It was one of the stranger meetings I've ever attended. Morrie wasn't happy with me and began to berate Hasselmo for one thing and another. He let it slip that Carlson was jealous of the close relationship Texas Gov. George W. Bush had with the president of the University of Texas—a tidbit that would serve me well a year later, when Hasselmo's successor arrived from the University of Texas. I took the criticism without much reaction until Anderson said that after seven years in office, Hasselmo was coasting as the university's president.

I couldn't let that pass. "That's baloney. This guy is working as hard as he ever has," I said. I started to tell Morrie about Hasselmo's efforts to make the university easier for undergraduates to navigate. Then the phone rang. I sensed that the call was important and offered to step out. "Yes, if you please," he said. I went out and stood in the corridor. And stood. The time that elapsed was much more than should have been needed for a phone conversation. Nobody said a word to me. I finally slunk away. I had never been dismissed from a meeting in that fashion before.

I WAS PROUD TO SUPPORT NILS—and not just because the institution needed a boost in reputation as it sought a new president. Many gains had been made on his watch. The academic quality of incoming students was up substantially as was the five-year graduation rate. Class sizes were down. The share of classes taught by professors rather than teaching assistants was up. More students were living on campus. Research funding had doubled; annual donations from private sources had tripled. He helped the university overcome its reputation for being "customer unfriendly." It was a shame that a controversy over tenure had obscured that record, even within the university community.

Beyond that, I thoroughly enjoyed Nils Hasselmo. I discovered that he was vigorous, determined, and decisive. He was Swedish by birth and possessed enough European formality to come across as reserved or a little stiff to some Minnesotans, but I found him delightful company. He deserves more credit in university annals than he was afforded while he served.

A FEW WEEKS AFTER I STARTED at the university, interim provost and physicist Marvin Marshak appeared at the door of my office in Morrill Hall. "Come with me," he said. "I want you to see why you're here."

Off we went to a freshman orientation session at the College of Science and Engineering. A large group of new students were assembled in an auditorium. As I watched, the session ended, and Marshak took about thirty of the students to a classroom for a discussion. I tagged along.

"What's the most important thing about a university education?" he asked the students. A few students offered some answers.

He picked up on one of them and emphasized it: "Getting involved. That's the key. Work with your fellow students. Be a participant. This is why you're here. Get to know your professors. What's another word for that? Sucking up. Go see your professors and teaching assistants. Don't be afraid to do that. It makes a difference. Go in, ask questions, get yourself identified." His message couldn't be mistaken and could not have been more important.

My most important contribution as a university official may have come in December 1996, as the search for Hasselmo's successor came to a head. Gerald Christenson, a very able public servant and educator who ended his career as chancellor of the Minnesota community college system, was the head of the search committee. He was politically adroit, but the atmosphere that surrounded the university administration at the time seemed to invite potshots. Some members of the search committee, including Medtronic board chair Win Wallin, publicly criticized the search process as insufficiently inclusive. Then on December 6—the Friday before scheduled campus visits by the search committee's three finalists—two of the three withdrew their candidacies. Gov. Arne Carlson promptly declared the search a bust and called for its suspension. Mark Yudof, a vice president at the University of Texas, was still scheduled to visit the Twin Cities campus on December 10. I consulted with Marvin Marshak. We agreed that I should call Yudof and make sure he was still willing to come. I had standing to make the call because Yudof and I had become acquainted by telephone a few weeks earlier. I had been identified to him as a knowledgeable administration insider and former business executive who was also somewhat independent and had no desire to become a permanent employee. On that basis, he called me to talk about the university's strengths and weaknesses. He was still an eager candidate, he assured me when I reached him. I told him that the other two finalists had dropped out, then asked, "What will you do if the search process is suspended?"

"If that happens, I'm history," he told me. It's what I expected he would say.

Marshak and I then called the chair of the Board of Regents, Tom Reagan, at his home in northeastern Minnesota. Reagan was on the edge of abandoning the process. I shared Yudof's message with him, along with my opinion: "You've got a good guy here. You ought to simply say you're looking forward to Yudof's visit and let him come." We persuaded him. He asked me to write a brief statement to that effect, which was released to the news media. (Meanwhile, search committee chair Gerry Christenson was on the phone to Lori Sturdevant of the *Star Tribune* editorial board. The result was a strongly worded editorial in the December 9 edition headlined, "Let Yudof come.")

In my opinion, if the regents had followed Carlson's advice and abandoned the search at that juncture, they would still be looking for an appropriately qualified new president today. It would have been a terrible mistake.

I FLEW TO AUSTIN, TEXAS, early one Saturday morning to meet with Yudof soon after his selection as the next university president. I went directly to his office at the University of Texas. He offered me a cup of coffee, which sounded good after my early morning flight. The coffee machine was perched atop a stack of books and papers in his office. He turned it on, and we went back to our conversation. Before long, I heard the sound of hissing and gurgling and smelled burned coffee. He was making an awful mess. It was clear that his many skills did not include those of a barista.

YUDOF BECAME THE UNIVERSITY'S PRESIDENT on July 1, 1997. He and I clicked from the beginning. My relationship with him was in part as staffer, Dutch uncle, and father figure. I gave him advice, which he accepted because he knew I had no agenda or motive other than to see him succeed for the university's sake.

"You're a Philadelphia lawyer who spent twenty-five years in Texas. That's enough to make Minnesotans leery or suspect," I told him. "You need to get out and meet Minnesotans—not just respond to invitations but get out with your own agenda and send a strong message." He agreed. With the help of my chief of staff Kathy Yaeger, we used the Extension Service to set up a series of events around the state.

Yudof was marvelous at those meetings. He was warm, witty, and sincere in asking for Minnesotans to rally around their flagship university. He had his own idea for a publicity gimmick. He liked to eat pancakes and let it be known that he was on a personal quest to find the perfect Minnesota pancakes. Before long, he was inundated with pancake recipes, invitations, and recommendations. Food writers at Minnesota newspapers devoted columns to his quest. Overnight in Minnesota eyes, he went from being a stranger to a friend.

I didn't advise him about pancakes, but I had other tips he took to heart. "When you're listening and not talking, don't look bored," I urged. "They're all looking at you." Don't complain too much about Minnesota winters. You're a Minnesotan now, and Minnesotans take winter in stride.

I saw to it that Judy Yudof was escorted in unfamiliar places and introduced when she was in attendance with a crowd. I thought that was the decent Minnesota way to do things. The Yudofs later told me that those gestures helped convince them that I sincerely wanted them to succeed.

Yudof would introduce me, too. "Tom's the only one on the university staff who was present in 1849 when the territorial legislature decided that the prison would be in Stillwater and the university in Minneapolis," he'd say.

I convinced Mark and Judy Yudof to dress in costumes and distribute candy to trick-or-treaters at Halloween. We provided a costume for him to use. He wore it in good spirits and seemed to enjoy himself. Afterward, though, he muttered to me, "Don't expect me to ever wear tights again."

NOT LONG AFTERWARD, Yudof was invited to join the TCF Bank board of directors. He was interested in accepting. At his previous academic post, the University of Texas, it was not uncommon for presidents to serve on local corporate boards. It would be a precedent here and probably not well received, I advised him. The board chair at TCF was Bill Cooper, who also served as chair of the Minnesota Republican Party. Yudof ought not be associated with partisan politics, I maintained. Besides, the Republican Party was arguing for "no new taxes" and state spending restraint, which conflicted with his call for the Legislature to boost funding for higher education. I was so intent on quickly blocking what I considered a potential misstep that I composed my argument as an e-mail and sent it directly to Yudof. It was the first time I'd ever used e-mail.

He responded with a phone call. "Come to my office" and discuss the matter, he said. By the time I arrived, he had made up his mind. "You're right," he told me. "I can't do this." We chatted for only a few minutes more. When I left the president's inner office, there in the outer office was Bill Cooper, waiting for Yudof's response to his invitation. I learned the value of e-mail that day.

I LEFT MORRILL HALL and returned to the ranks of the loyal alumni after a very successful legislative session in 1998. Mark Dienhart's departure as athletic director in 1999 in the aftermath of an academic cheating scandal saddened me. Basketball coach Clem Haskins and vice president for student affairs and athletics McKinley Boston were sacked, and Dienhart resigned under heavy pressure. Dienhart had no discernible ties to the academic misconduct that had been discovered in the basketball program, but Yudof evidently believed that a problem of the magnitude of this scandal warranted a top-to-bottom housecleaning.

I much admired Dienhart, as I had his father, who had been valedictorian of my 1938 class at Washburn High School. In my book, Mark Dienhart's integrity is without question. He wound up at U.S. Bank, then at the University of St. Thomas as executive vice president. On his watch, he raised a stunning $515 million for that institution. Today he heads the Schulze Family Foundation, established by the founder of Best Buy Corp. The University of Minnesota lost a great talent when he departed.

I URGED YUDOF to give Sid Hartman some attention. Sid is fundamentally a great loyalist to the university and is in a position to be helpful to a new administration, I counseled. Yudof took my words to heart and put on a charm offensive that would melt a block of ice. It wasn't long before Sid was writing in the *Star Tribune* that Mark Yudof was the greatest president in University of Minnesota history.

When Yudof resigned in 2002 to become chancellor of the University of Texas, Sid hosted a farewell party for him. I don't recall him doing that for any other university official. Sid invited about thirty people to Vescio's Restaurant in Dinkytown, including Arlene and me. We arrived a bit early and were greeted by our genial host with the advisory, "Swain, you're the program." It was the first I'd heard that there would be a program, let alone that I would speak.

The other guests arrived. We ate dinner. Then Sid started the program by presenting Yudof with a gift—a Sid Hartman bobble-head doll. Once that touching formality was dispensed with, Sid announced, "We don't have much of a program tonight. Here he is, Tom Swain." One doesn't quite know what to say after an introduction like that.

SANDRA GARDEBRING SUCCEEDED ME in 1998 as the university's vice president for institutional relations. She was a versatile and able public servant whose Minnesota career included three years as a justice on the Minnesota Supreme Court. California Polytechnic Institute lured her away in 2004. It was located in San Luis Opispo, where she and her husband Paul Ogren owned a home and were planning to retire. What we didn't know when she left was that she was ailing with a rare form of cancer. She died in 2010, far too soon, at age sixty-three.

Her departure created a vacancy in my old office. Yudof's successor, Robert Bruininks, decided to fill it temporarily with a familiar figure—me. Bruininks had been academic provost under Yudof and had been on the faculty for thirty-five years. He and I were well acquainted. I had a rare opportunity to be a close-at-hand adviser with a third university president.

Bruininks tried to elevate Minnesotans' sense of the institution's potential for greatness. He spoke frequently in the year I was back on campus about making the University of Minnesota one of the top three public research universities in the world. I counseled moderation in that rhetoric. This was at a time when the state grappled with recurring money trouble and responded by squeezing appropriations for higher education. If the university could make modest gains in national ranking during that period, it would be doing well.

I enjoyed working with Bruininks. He was a gentleman who treated his entire staff with respect, and they returned the sentiment. A fine sense of teamwork prevailed in his administration. And what a talented team he had, too: Donna Peterson as our lobbyist, J. Peter Zetterberg and Richard Pfutzenreuter at finance, Kathleen O'Brien at university services, Joel Maturi as athletic director, Tom Sullivan as academic provost are only a few of the people on his team who excelled at what they did. My second stint as a university vice president lasted a few months shy of a year. It was a privilege to be there.

CHAPTER 26

Questions

MY HABIT IS TO ASK A LOT OF QUESTIONS in just about every setting. It's my way of showing interest in people, keeping a conversation lively and substantive, and eliciting information that can aid decision making. Sometimes my question is just "Help me understand . . . " or "Say more, please." Often that's all it takes to get to the heart of matters. On various volunteer boards and committees, I may not have been the biggest donor or the most prominent name, but maybe I contributed by helping the group become better informed.

One of those panels was created by the Lawyers' Professional Responsibility Board. It adjudicates complaints about lawyers' conduct and conducts programs promoting adherence to ethical standards in the practice of law. I gravitated to efforts to sustain the quality of the Minnesota judicial system, which I believe is the best in the nation. That idea was behind my work for twenty-eight years on the state Compensation Council, which recommends salaries in all three branches of state government, and on Gov. Arne Carlson's Judicial Merit Selection Commission. I was also a citizen member of the judicial branch's disciplinary panel. Chief Justice Lorie Skjerven Gildea sent me a nice letter in 2012 saying that no other private citizen had been as involved in the work of the Minnesota courts.

The Lawyers' Professional Responsibility Board panel on which I served in the 1980s consisted of two attorneys and me. We heard a complaint against an attorney in a major firm. He was able to marshal considerable legal talent to defend him. One witness on his behalf was U.S. District Judge Miles Lord—a former Minnesota attorney general who was then one of the most prominent, colorful, and controversial judges in any federal courthouse in the country. Lord had plenty of experience asking sharp questions in his own

Bob and Tom Swain, 1925.

Earl Swain and his sons, circa 1929. From left: Bob, Jerry, Joe, and Tom.

Tom Swain, circa 1933.

Four grown brothers, circa 1950: Bob, Joe, Tom, and Jerry.

GIs outside squad tent on Okinawa. Ten men occupied each tent, and Tom is second from left in the back row. Typhoon Louise flattened the tent in October 1945.

Corporal Swain, Pyote, Texas, 1943.

The 1934 Plymouth outside the Swains' first house, 5420 Logan Avenue South, Minneapolis.

Arlene with her sister Dorothy before her wedding at Incarnation Catholic Church in Minneapolis, June 19, 1947.

Bride and groom with their mothers at the wedding reception at the McWilliams home, June 19, 1947.

Swain at the University of Minnesota ticket office, 1948.

Swain (*right*) with Coach Bierman outside the team's hotel at a Golden Gophers game in Seattle in 1950.

A billboard featuring the Indian sculpture as a symbol of St. Paul. During the summer, the commercial advertising would be replaced by a slogan promoting "St. Paul's Indian." From left, unidentified Naegele manager, Swain, Naegele president Walter Broich, and Jerry Settergren.

Swain at the St. Paul convention bureau, 1952.

Delmar Hagen of Pembina, Minnesota, brought his ox and ancient oxcart to Statehood Week in St. Paul in May 1958 to recreate the midsummer oxcart treks from the Red River Valley to St. Paul that were routine in the 1850s.

The Centennial Train crosses the Stone Arch Bridge in Minneapolis.

Minnesota Centennial Showboat on the Mississippi River, 1958.

This photograph of John Foster Dulles and Judy Garland was published on the front page of the *Minneapolis Tribune* on May 12, 1958, and upset Judy Garland.

Tom's duties as state commissioner of business development in 1962 took him around the state and often included interviews with local journalists. This Duluth TV reporter spoke with him as he surveyed that city from a downtown rooftop.

Swain family, circa 1965. (*Seated, from left*) Tom, Mary, and Barbara; (*behind them*) Arlene, Spike (Thomas M.), and Jo Anne.

Jo Anne and Patrick Murray's wedding day, December 31, 1966.

TOM SWAIN, BACK FROM TALKS WITH N. VIETS, WITH DAUGHTER JOANNE
Her Husband, Capt. Patrick Murray, Has Been Missing 20 Months Since Air Mission

Join Peace Groups, N. Viets Told Swain

By LEWIS PATTERSON
Staff Writer

North Vietnamese dele-
gates to the Paris peace
talks urged him and then

parently meaning if they
were alive.

Despite this, Swain said,
he has "hopes" that more
information will be forth-

namese told them to "con-
a'ong and talk" after th
made contact in Paris I
said it was very difficult
explain to the North Vi

Minnesota reporters—and Jo Anne—were waiting when Swain returned from Paris in October 1969. This story appeared in the *St. Paul Pioneer Press.*

Gubernatorial candidate Elmer L. Andersen visits with supporters during a campaign stop, circa 1960.

Breaks were rare for staffers in Governor Elmer Andersen's lean operation. But so is a February day in Minnesota warm enough for ice cream.
Tom and Elmer took advantage of an unseasonably warm day in February
1961 to pose for a tourism promotion photograph. The message: winters in
Minnesota aren't all bad.

Tom and Arlene join a salute to U.S. Senator Dave Durenberger as he prepares to leave the Senate in 1994.

The cover of Swain's 2008 Lilydale mayoral campaign brochure.

Tom with Goldie Gopher.

Swain with University of Minnesota president Mark Yudof at a reception at Eastcliff, the university president's home, soon after Yudof took office in July 1997.

The Swain grandchildren: McWilliam "Will" Goldstein, Drew Swain, Lisa Johnson, Andrea Goldstein, Merritt Swain, Pat Swain, and Nick Goldstein, July 4, 1990.

Barbara's wedding in 1984 brought all of Arlene's sisters together. Standing, from left, daughter Mary Goldstein, sisters Mildred, Lois, Marjorie, and Marilyn, daughter-in-law Laura Swain, and daughter Jo Anne Driscoll; seated are Arlene, bride Barbara, and Arlene's sister Dorothy.

Tom and Arlene Swain.

courtroom. That didn't stifle me. I stuck with my usual pattern of asking a lot of questions—although it did occur to me at some point during our exchange, "Here I am, interrogating a federal judge. This is an odd situation!"

Lord committed the cardinal sin of witnesses. He just kept talking. Witnesses in adversarial proceedings are coached to keep their answers as direct and succinct as possible, revealing nothing more than was asked. Lord surely had heard that advice and likely had given it himself, but he evidently couldn't apply it to himself. I watched the increasingly visible discomfort of the lead attorney defending the fellow who stood accused before us. He couldn't get Lord to shut up.

AS CHAIR OF THE Minnesota Health Care Commission from 1992 to 1995, I was at a bit of a disadvantage. Most of the twenty-five other commission members made their livelihoods in some aspect of the health care industry. I knew something about one small sliver of that industry, medical malpractice insurance. Otherwise, I was an interested nonexpert. My job was to bring the group to agreement on recommendations to the Legislature and governor.

Asking plenty of questions helped me do that job. My other tactic was to listen for the emergence of a consensus and then try to articulate that point of agreement. "I'm no expert," I'd generally say, "but I think we're coming together this way . . ." Michael Scandrett, our commission's executive director, told me recently—twenty years after we worked together—that he'd listen expectantly at each meeting for the moment when I'd say, "I'm no expert, but . . ." He knew that when I said that, we were on the verge of a decision.

KATHY YAEGER WAS MY MARVELOUS CHIEF OF STAFF at the University of Minnesota when I was vice president for institutional relations. She was an exceedingly able organizer, writer, and adviser and did a lot to keep me out of trouble. At my first university executive council meeting in 1996, she sat behind me and paid close attention to matters under discussion that would require my subsequent attention. During that meeting, she kept track of how many questions I asked and stopped counting at ten.

"Why do you ask so many questions?" she asked me afterward.

"Because I need the answers," I said.

My approach at university meetings, at least initially, was to keep quiet when I wasn't asking questions. I'm not intimidated by business executives, politicians, or stellar athletes, but I have respect verging on awe for teachers. There's a culture at any good university of respect for professors. I wasn't one to come from outside and expect that to change. I wanted to understand how to operate within that culture and hoped that I could win the respect of the people there.

ONCE I WENT to an Elder Learning Institute class and dozed off, long enough for the teacher to notice. After a brief snooze, I awoke and promptly asked a question.

"You've been asleep," the teacher correctly observed. "How do you know I haven't already answered that question?"

"Well, a fella's got to take a few chances in life," I replied.

HERE'S A TIP: when you first meet someone, ask where that person started in life. I almost always do, and I like the results. The question conveys the message, "I'm interested in you." Most people like answering. Sometimes there's a crossroads there, a connection we might have and can discuss. Their answers help me remember them, should we meet again. And to be remembered later, after only a brief exchange at a first meeting, is a flattering experience for most people.

CHAPTER 27

Still a Republican

IN 1978 I was an early backer of Dave Durenberger—for governor. Durenberger might be considered part of the Elmer Andersen wing of the Republican Party. He's an attorney and former U.S. Army intelligence officer who was chief of staff for Gov. Harold LeVander from 1967 to 1970 and then went to work for Elmer at H. B. Fuller Co., where he held a number of positions, including legal counsel. I'm not sure when I became aware of him, but I'm sure Elmer figures in our connection.

It irked me when party leaders decided that retiring U.S. Rep. Al Quie, not Durenberger, should be the Republican candidate for governor that year and that Durenberger should switch to the U.S. Senate race. I had nothing against Quie. He's a fine man and has given this state distinguished service. But Durenberger's career seemed to point toward being governor.

I was among the reluctant members of Durenberger's campaign committee when he announced his candidacy for the U.S. Senate seat that had been held by Hubert Humphrey. But his bid was not hopeless, as it would have been if Humphrey still occupied it. Humphrey had died in January 1978, and the seat had been filled by his widow, Muriel, who decided not to seek election in her own right.

Humphrey always acknowledged me as his distant cousin at public occasions when we were together. I presented him with the Distinguished Citizen Award of the Minnesota Chapter of the Public Relations Society of America in 1969, a year he was out of office. He'd been defeated in his presidential bid in 1968 and was not yet back in the U.S. Senate, to which he returned in January 1971. That day Hubert said of me that being related to him "is one of the burdens he has had to carry through his life. It helped build character."

I wasn't much in touch with Hubert in his last years. He had disappointed me with his role in the I-35 shoddy workmanship accusations that contributed to Elmer's narrow reelection defeat in 1962. I noted a news story in 1974 or 1975 when one of the notorious Nixon dirty tricksters, Donald Segretti, was released from prison. He apologized to Humphrey for faked letters he wrote on purloined Senate stationery accusing Humphrey of all manner of misdeeds and outrageous comments. Segretti's apology inspired a letter from me to Hubert. Wouldn't this be a fine time for you to write a letter of apology to Elmer Andersen? I asked. It was the only letter I ever sent to him that did not bring a reply. I learned much later via third-hand sources that days before he died in January 1978, Hubert told a visiting priest that creating a "scandal" out of trivial I-35 construction flaws in 1962 was his greatest regret in his thirty-four-year political career. I'm glad Elmer eventually heard that roundabout report.

The DFL nomination for the U.S. Senate in 1978 was up for grabs in a party that was sorely divided between metro liberals and more conservative outstaters. The flashpoints were abortion, guns, and environmental protection—specifically in the Boundary Waters Canoe Area, a million-acre wilderness in northeastern Minnesota administered by the U.S. Forest Service. The favored candidate of DFL liberals was U.S. Rep. Don Fraser, who had been the House sponsor of legislation limiting motors in the BWCA to only a handful of places. He won party endorsement but was facing a no-holds-barred challenge in the DFL primary from wealthy Minneapolis business mogul Robert Short. Short won in a bitter and close contest that, on the morning after the primary, left a good share of Twin Cities liberals interested in getting to know the Republican candidate for the seat.

They found an appealing alternative in Durenberger. He led the ticket in a Republican sweep. I had played only a minor role in his campaign, but he always treated me with great kindness and deference, making time for me whenever business at The St. Paul Companies took me to Washington. He took an independent look at any insurance matter we brought to his attention. He didn't always agree with us, but when he didn't, he had clear and logical reasons. I thought he did an excellent job, becoming an even-handed, fair-minded authority on health care and U.S. intelligence. It was a disappointment when he chose not to run again in 1994.

THE REPUBLICAN PARTY'S battle cry has long been "no new taxes." But this Republican took umbrage in early 1979 when, on a homeward-bound flight from Phoenix, a Western Airlines pilot announced that we were on board flight so-and-so "to Minnesota, the land of 10,000 taxes." The next day, January 10, I wrote a letter to the airline's president, Dominic Renda, in Los Angeles. "It was unseemly and inappropriate, in my judgment, for a Western employee, and certainly not one of your lower-paid employees, to editorialize in this fashion. Is it Western policy to criticize Minnesota's tax levels?" I noted that while per capita taxes are high in Minnesota, they are higher in California, where the airline was headquartered. I requested a reply—and copied newly inaugurated Republican Gov. Al Quie and St. Paul Chamber of Commerce executive vice president Amos Martin. Quie promptly dropped me a note asking me to share any reply I might receive.

I waited, and waited. Patience is not my strong suit. On February 8, I wrote Renda again. "In our company, we have a policy that all consumer complaints must be acknowledged within 48 hours of receipt. . . . Furthermore, we expect satisfactory answer be provided complainant within three weeks. What's your policy?" I asked. "Am I to assume that no response is intended?"

The response that finally came was dated February 9, over the signature of the airline's regional vice president, Lynn Zumbrunnen. He described the pilot's remark as "the unfortunate announcement" and soothed that it "does not reflect in any way our views of the quality of life which we all enjoy in Minnesota." He apologized. "We feel, as you do, that Minnesota is an excellent place to live and work."

It was good to see that sentiment in black and white on a major corporation's letterhead. The business lobby at the Capitol in 1979 had raised the intensity and volume of their complaints about Minnesota's allegedly chilly business climate. It's now clear that was part of a national strategy on the part of business leaders, begun during the Nixon administration.

I didn't think then and I don't think now that complaints about Minnesota's business climate were justified. High state tax rates have not been this state's undoing. Rather, they've paid for the education, infrastructure, law enforcement, and social services that undergird a high quality of life. Minnesota continues to lead the nation in almost any measure of economic progress. There are retirees who leave for states with lower taxes only to return as they age and want to take advantage of Minnesota's extraordinary health care system—made possible in large measure by government investment and support. I've noticed that the new Greater MSP business organization is making a point of bragging about the advantages this region offers to all its residents, employers included. That's the emphasis I'd like to see from all of the state's business groups.

I FAITHFULLY ATTENDED Republican precinct caucuses until 2014 and then lapsed only because I had very recently moved to my apartment. But already in the mid-1990s, Arlene was getting tired of going to Republican caucuses. She was never as consistent a Republican voter as I had been.

In 1992, a year when Minnesota Republicans were sorely divided into moderate and conservative camps, we caucused at Sibley High School. Arlene sat on the opposite side of the room from me. I asked her why she didn't want to sit with me. "You talk too much," she said. She's never been one to sugarcoat her feedback on my conduct.

Undeterred, I chimed in frequently as the convener, Donald Bartho, a Lilydale City Council member, began the proceedings. For example, when he asked for nominations for precinct chairman and chairwoman, I suggested, "Let's find out first if anyone wants those jobs." Ed Stringer, who at that time was Gov. Arne Carlson's chief of staff, was in attendance. He said he'd like to chair the precinct. He was quickly elected, as was the daughter of Lilydale Mayor Edward Mullarky. The convener, a very conservative fellow, may not have appreciated my help. Both Stringer and the Mullarkys were allied with Carlson and progressive Republican politics. At least I was trying to expedite things.

The next issue was the election of four delegates and four alternates to the Republican legislative district convention. I had some suggestions for speeding that along too. Then we started nominations—and somebody nominated me. Someone else nominated Fred Lanners, a retired CEO of Ecolab and the former boss of Jon Grunseth, the ill-fated GOP conservative who had been Arne Carlson's GOP rival for governor in 1990. Lanners was my neighbor.

After all the nominations had been made, I said, "Let's find out how everybody stands on the issues." I spoke in support of President George H. W. Bush, who was facing a tough reelection fight that year, and of Governor Carlson. Lanners then asked, "Where do you stand on abortion?" I gave a pro-choice speech that my daughters likely would have approved but my listeners didn't warmly receive.

Lanners then explained his view. At one time, he said, he was willing to accept legal abortion in cases of rape and incest, but he had come around to preferring an all-out ban on the procedure. "I just can't make those distinctions," he said. The room erupted in applause.

Ballots were shortly cast; tellers were dispatched to count; they returned to announce a tie for fourth place, between me and convener Donald Bartho. We flipped a coin; he called it true. He became a delegate, and I was the alternate.

On the way home, I asked Arlene whether she had voted for me.

"No," she said as if it were a point of pride. "I only voted for women candidates."

One might say that a conservative male was sent to represent Lilydale at the Republican State Convention that year because Arlene Swain was a devoted feminist. That's perverse—and that's politics.

I'VE SUPPORTED the Independence Party candidates for governor in the last two elections—Peter Hutchinson in 2006, and Tom Horner in 2010. In 2002, I supported the eventual winner, Tim Pawlenty, in the early going but ultimately voted for Independence candidate Tim Penny.

I still consider myself a Republican. What Republicans traditionally stand for is what I support: fiscal responsibility, civil rights, free enterprise, quality public services. Their candidates through the years mostly struck me as honorable people who were easy to support. I haven't been happy with my party lately. But once you belong to something, you belong. Today's Republicans can't take that away from me.

A few weeks after Pawlenty was elected governor in 2002, I wrote him a note of "congratulations, confession, concern, and best wishes." The confession was my vote for Penny. The concern was that he had boxed himself into a policy corner with a "no new taxes" pledge and that he would be unwilling or unable to compromise as a result. "Practical politics in the final analysis is holding to your principles but seeking acceptable compromise on issues," I counseled. "Financing appropriate state government services in the next few years will be a formidable challenge. Some think paring off the fat can cure all. You have been around long enough to know that there just isn't that much fat. Health care commitments will expand; education needs to build our future must be nourished. Open minds are imperative."

Pawlenty responded with a form letter. His actions as governor showed that my concerns were well founded. When I wrote again expressing similar concerns after the 2006 election—in which I was a cochair of Hutchinson's campaign committee—the reelected governor did not bother to send a reply. What I wrote to Pawlenty in 2002 I'd say to Republican candidates today: "If ever you feel that I can be of assistance, don't hesitate to ask."

CHAPTER 28

Show 'Em the Money

DETERMINING THE RIGHTFUL COMPENSATION for elected officials has always been a matter of political delicacy in Minnesota. The state constitution acknowledges as much, specifying that any pay raise for legislators enacted in one session cannot go into effect until after the next election, giving a new Legislature the chance to repeal it. That gives voters de facto veto power over pay raises. But it also means that legislators have skimped on compensation for themselves and by extension governors, other executive branch officials, and judges. That might be good politics in the short term, but it's a bad way to run a high-quality state in the long run. Its consequence is that people of talent tend to spurn state service because the income sacrifice that it would require is too great.

I saw that play out in dramatic fashion when one of Gov. Elmer Andersen's best judicial appointments, Supreme Court Justice Robert Sheran, left the high court seven years after Elmer appointed him. When he was appointed, his annual salary was $20,000; by 1970, it had climbed to $26,000. That wasn't enough. With seven children, several of college age, he simply couldn't afford to serve. Fortunately a few years later, when Sheran's children were older and the court's chief justice salary was $40,000 a year, Gov. Wendell Anderson was wise enough to bring him back as chief justice. He was one of the state's best.

Sheran was on my mind as I agreed to join the State Compensation Council in 1987, soon after I retired from The St. Paul Companies. I stayed with the sixteen-member council for the next twenty-five years, a good many of them as its chair. As required by a 1983 law, our council assembled every odd-numbered year to make a recommendation to the Legislature by March 15. In many of those years, we were officially thanked, then ignored.

Legislators have been paid $31,140 per year since 1999, when they received a 5 percent increase, the first in many years. Three leaders in each legislative chamber are presumed to serve full-time and receive 40 percent more. The governor's salary was stuck at $120,000 from 1998 until 2014, when it rose to nearly $124,000. The governor's salary might be deemed adequate for a four-year "temp" job, especially since it comes with a house, a car, and a driver. But until 2013, no state agency head's salary could exceed 95 percent of the governor's. The 2013 Legislature wisely raised that cap to 133 percent of the governor's pay. The highly skilled experts and managers who run a $20 billion per year operation deserve at least that much. The state's ability to lure and keep top talent suffers if they don't.

Legislators' pay is supplemented by per diem, an old-fashioned means of reimbursing expenses, a means I see as obfuscation. During legislative sessions, up to seven days a week, House members can claim up to $77 per day, senators up to $96. Many don't claim the full amount, and those who do are subjects of suspicion. For those who must pay rent in the Twin Cities and either relocate their families or commute to the far corners of the state on weekends for half of each year, those sums are not extravagant. For others, per diem is a salary supplement that has little connection to actual work-related expenses.

The compensation council existed to take some of the taint of self-dealing away from elected officials who favor higher pay. We provided an independent examination of state government's pay structure and took our findings to the public. When we recommended increases, as we almost always did, we were offering legislators and governors political cover for doing the right thing. They often rejected it, for reasons that became increasingly hard to understand.

State Rep. Ron Kraus, an Albert Lea Republican, may have spoken for many when he sent me a rebuke in 1995. His letter said the council's recommendations "got the attention they deserved—none!" from the 1995 Legislature. Kraus was an owner of Dairy Queens and convenience stores in rural Minnesota and Iowa. He announced his intention to introduce legislation reconstituting our council to include more "hard-working" people. "Lower- and middle-class, hard-working people from across the state may look differently upon wages than you do," Kraus wrote in May, shortly after that year's session adjourned without acting on our recommendations.

Kraus, a freshman legislator, didn't make good on his threat to change our council's composition. Meanwhile, my file of news clippings about Minnesota officials leaving public service to go to other states or the private sector kept growing.

In 2009—as the state faced a major recession and a massive budget deficit—the council changed its approach. Noting that our recommendations had been ignored for ten years, we did not recommend salary increases that year. Rather, we suggested that a constitutional amendment be placed on the 2010 ballot giving the State Compensation Council full authority to raise salaries. That idea languished too, for a time. But it was picked up in 2013 when an attempt by DFL leaders to raise salaries stalled in the House. The compromise was a constitutional amendment along the lines we proposed. It will be on the ballot in 2016. I'll be urging a yes vote.

CHAPTER 29

Mr. Mayor

L ILYDALE, the small community just across the Mississippi River and the Interstate 35E bridge from St. Paul, became our home in 1981 and the focus of my public service in later years. Arlene chose the location after we'd spent ten years in Stillwater. She wanted to be closer to grandchildren and city activities. The townhouse she selected suited us well and was our home for thirty-three years, longer than we lived anywhere else.

In 1996, new Lilydale Mayor Ed Mullarky, whom I knew to be a Republican of moderate mindset like my own, asked me to chair the Lilydale Planning Commission. I figured, how hard could that be? Lilydale had only 552 people in the 2000 census, and its median age was sixty-two. It has only five houses; the rest of its residential properties are apartments, town houses, and condominiums, strung along the river. All of the city's residences have been built since a flood in 1965 wiped out the original town site. None of its households lived below the poverty line. Planning in Lilydale shouldn't be that strenuous, I reasoned as I accepted the job.

Soon after I arrived, the commission's approval was sought for a proposed residential and retail development, Stonebridge. On the site of a former sand quarry and mobile cement plant, Stonebridge is atop a bluff on the south side of the Mississippi River, which meant that the jurisdictions that had some say over the project's scope and design included the state Department of Natural Resources. The developer was St. Paul–based Rancone Development Co., headed by gregarious, high-spirited Gene Rancone. He sought the city's permission to divert its property taxes to the civic infrastructure the project required via the mechanism known as tax increment financing, or TIF. It was a big request for a small city. I was in for an interesting time.

Stonebridge was the best of several development proposals we considered for the site. I favored the project, as did most of the community. It meant seventy-seven more residential units and 45,000 square feet of additional retail space—a major expansion of our property tax base. But the proposed TIF arrangement would delay the time when Stonebridge's taxes could be used for general purposes. That was controversial. The project also had detractors among a few retailers, who didn't welcome the competition it would bring. And state regulators were concerned about the project's impact on the river and bluff below. They had requirements governing a project's height, landscaping, paved surfaces, and setback from the bluff. Those concerns had to be satisfied before the planning commission could give a green light to Stonebridge.

Rancone was an experienced developer who had done major projects on both sides of the Twin Cities, but he had never before had to deal with the DNR. Sometimes at planning commission meetings, his temper would get the better of him. This time, as the guy holding the gavel at meetings, I intended to do what I could to keep the meetings orderly and the project advancing. When I detected that Rancone was getting hot under the collar, I'd call for a brief recess. I'd quietly say a few soothing words to Rancone or nudge the DNR people in attendance to extend an olive branch to the developer.

It worked. Stonebridge opened in 2001. Rancone told me later it never would have happened if I hadn't helped him keep his cool. That was a stretch, but close.

MULLARKY RETIRED as mayor in 2006, at age ninety-one, and moved in with his daughter in another city. Of the city council members who might have succeeded him, one died, one was moving away, and one was ailing with cancer. "You're the only one who can do it," said the people who asked me to run. I ran for mayor without opposition, at age eighty-five—representing a youth movement by Lilydale standards.

I thought I knew quite a bit about the city's operations after serving for eleven years on the planning commission. That's why it came as a shock to learn after the election that Lilydale's expenses had exceeded its revenues in each of the past seven years, and the town was $230,000 in debt. That may not sound like much. But in a community of about seven hundred mostly senior citizens, it was about half of our annual operating budget.

That much debt was unacceptable. But so would have been a tax increase big enough to fill the gap. Lilydale had just raised its levy a politically unpopular 37 percent in 2006 and 17 percent in 2007. Many senior citizens live on incomes that are fixed, or nearly so. They can't handle big year-to-year increases in property taxes.

We launched a cost-cutting campaign. I renegotiated our contract with neighboring Mendota Heights for police services, shaving $30,000 off our annual costs. Our annual legal budget was trimmed by $20,000. Fees for liquor licenses and other annual business permits were increased, raising $8,000 per year. Our short- and long-term debt was refinanced, saving $5,000 in debt service the first year and more in later years. The winter thermostat went down and the summer one went up at City Hall. Lights went off in the City Hall parking lot on nights when no meetings were scheduled, saving $100 per month. I even promoted the slogan, "Floss, Don't Flush." Flushed dental floss gets into our sewer treatment facility, causing costly damage to its pump and filters.

Those were moves in the right direction, but they weren't enough. Our resolve not to raise taxes cracked. The City Council agreed to a 2.7 percent levy increase for 2008, promising to dedicate the entire increase to debt reduction. That raised another $30,000 that year.

The sale of a 0.85-acre, undeveloped city-owned lot also looked appealing. It had been donated to the city some years earlier. Its sale would allow us to retire our debt with some one-time resources to spare, with which we could build a reserve fund or invest in other civic needs. All but one member of the City Council agreed with me. The one dissenter was Marilyn Lundberg.

Lundberg became my most persistent critic. She contended that the lot had been donated with the condition that it be used as a park or left undeveloped as open space. Our city attorney Michael O'Brien checked into the record of its transfer from a would-be developer to the city and found no agreement that it be used for park purposes. My contention was that the city had no need for it and that it was better used to add to the city's tax base. She responded by forming a protest group called Save the Upper Bluff.

Those of us favoring the sale prevailed but at an inopportune time—late 2007, the start of the Great Recession. The market collapsed, and the land was never sold. At one point, we reduced the price from $329,000 to $279,000—and Marilyn objected, saying that I did not have the authority to make that change. After I left office, the city took the lot off the market.

That was typical of the back-and-forth between Marilyn and me while I was mayor. I made some quick decisions in 2007 to bring the city's finances into order. She claimed I was not sufficiently collaborative. At one point, she accused me of violating the state's Open Meeting Law—a charge that collapsed upon investigation.

Marilyn recruited one of her allies, Kay Frye, a former high school guidance counselor, to run against me in 2008. Frye, sixty-four, had no political experience. But Lundberg did. Under her tutelage, Frye leveled charges against me that fell fairly wide of the truth. In the campaign's closing days, Frye's campaign dropped literature at Lilydale doors claiming that I was responsible for the city's excessive debt. It said that as planning commission chair, I'd "participated in decisions" to build an extravagant new City Hall, divert too much of the city's property tax revenue stream to Stonebridge via TIF, and backed development of the former Lilydale Tennis Club by an underfunded developer.

My supporters weren't about to let those false and misleading claims go unanswered, even though time was short. I had the backing of the other three City Council members—Robert Bullard, Anita Pampusch, and Warren Peterson—and Planning and Zoning Commission chair John Diehl. Over their signatures, we published a one-page fact sheet refuting each of her points. I had nothing to do with the decision to build a new City Hall—which cost about 65 percent of the amount Frye cited. Stonebridge residents—who would not be in Lilydale had the project not been approved—pay 100 percent of TIF receipts. And the tennis club sale to a developer who turned out to be underfunded was a private transaction that city government could not control or prevent.

I had a committed campaign crew who fanned out throughout

the town the night before the election, distributing our fact sheet. It concluded: "The Frye campaign's distribution of false and misleading statements four days before the election is a tactic that they may think is clever, but it destroys the collegiality in city governance. If that works in Lilydale, it will cause incalculable damage to our community."

I won reelection by a vote of 335–215, or 60.8 percent. That's a strong margin in any election these days. Yet for some time, it was difficult for me to understand how anybody could have voted against me. I thought I'd done a first-rate job. I'd been involved in politics for most of my adult life. But it was not until I was on the ballot myself in a contested election that I fully appreciated what candidates go through—how vulnerable they are to ill-informed criticism, how hard it can be to persevere in the face of unfair attacks. I came away from my 2008 election keenly aware that democracy asks a lot of those who are willing to serve. We ought to appreciate them more.

Lilydale's financial circumstances improved as the economy climbed out of recession. We were able to pay off the bonds for Stonebridge's improvements earlier than planned. That ended the Stonebridge tax increment financing district and brought its taxes into the city's general fund, leading to a significant cut in the city's share of its residents' property tax bills.

I ENJOYED MY CONNECTION with the businesses that today are most associated with the Stonebridge development, Buon Giorno restaurant and delicatessen, its related fine-dining Italian restaurant I Nonni, and its off-sale wine store. Restaurateur Frank Marchionda and I became good friends as he obtained liquor licenses for his businesses. Across the road from I Nonni is another liquor store that was prepared to mount a City Hall fight if Frank tried to install a full-scale liquor store at Stonebridge. We negotiated a truce that allowed Frank's off-sale business to consist entirely of Italian wines and grappa.

In most places in Minnesota, Frank would be obliged to keep the wine store and the deli separate, with separate entrances. One would be able to buy a glass or bottle of wine in the deli for consumption there, but not buy a bottle of wine in the deli to take home. That state regulation separating on- and off-sale liquor purchases does not apply in cities with populations of less than 1,000, I told Frank. Nothing prevented him from offering wine for carryout sale in the deli as well as in the wine store, I assured him. He didn't believe me. We argued for a year. He finally consulted his attorney, who said, "Swain is right." He now sells more off-sale wine in the deli than he does in the wine store.

Arlene's failing health factored into my decision not to seek a third term in 2010. I enjoyed being mayor. We encountered more problems than expected, but I think we dealt with them well. I had good support from colleagues. One of them, Anita Pampusch, the former president of St. Catherine University and of the Bush Foundation, succeeded me as mayor. She's a great public servant. The experience left me convinced that serving in local government is a fine way for retired people to make a continuing contribution to the places they love. Anita is demonstrating that, too.

CHAPTER 30

Things Change

I SHUDDERED when I came across a joke I used to tell when I gave speeches in the 1950s. It's one I would never tell today except to make this point: I've been party to a great societal change in respect and regard for women.

The bad joke: A boy complains to his father, "Mommy backed out of the garage and ran over my bike." Dad responds, "That will teach you to leave your bike on the front porch."

In my lifetime, women have gone from newly getting the right to vote—and seldom driving a car—to running major corporations and serving in every occupation. I applaud the change. I like to think that I was ready for it and that I responded with encouragement and support for the women in my life as it happened. But that awful joke suggests that even an enlightened guy like me had a lot to learn.

One of the ways I hope that I redeemed myself was in advancing the careers of bright young women. I was instrumental in making Patricia Johnson the first female president of the State Fund Mutual Insurance Co. and in hiring Karen Himle at The St. Paul Companies on a tight deadline, when she was on the verge of being transferred to Topeka, Kansas, by her former employer. Karen more than confirmed my trust, becoming the company's senior vice president for corporate and government affairs and eventually a vice president at the University of Minnesota, in the office I had previously led.

CHANGE IN THE STATUS OF WOMEN came on strong in the 1970s when I was at The St. Paul Companies. Women were rising in corporate ranks and were no longer willing to silently suffer abuse or sexual harassment on the job. I was one of the men in the company positioned to receive their complaints and was someone female employees trusted to give them a fair hearing. A high-ranking executive at one of our subsidiaries was accused of harassment. A generation earlier, his misconduct might have been overlooked. I was among those who argued that this time, it could not be. He wound up leaving the company.

One part of our changed norms about women involved the use of the term "women" rather than "girls." Calling grown women "girls" wasn't respectful and, by the mid-1970s, was also no longer socially acceptable. But I had trouble shedding the habit of saying "Hi, girls!" to a group of female coworkers I encountered at The St. Paul Companies each day, even though I would sometimes get a scowl in response.

Finally, I asked colleague Mary Pickard what she would like me to say instead. "Hi, women!" didn't seem right to me.

She replied, "Try, 'Hello, fellow key contributors!'"

ON AUGUST 24, 1994, about twenty female friends surprised me with a luncheon I'll never forget. At The St. Paul Hotel's Mayo Room under a banner reading "Women Who Appreciate Tom Swain," they saluted me for being their mentor and ally as they navigated their career paths. Arlene and my daughters and daughter-in-law were in on the surprise and were present too. Gov. Arne Carlson sent a proclamation in honor of the event. It was a grand day.

MINNESOTANS PLAYED SUCH A PROMINENT ROLE in the civil rights movement of the 1950s and 1960s in the United States that we tend to forget that we had segregation to overturn within our own state. I was involved in a small way in a move to desegregate fraternities at the University of Minnesota in 1953–54.

That year, the student leaders of my fraternity, Theta Chi, enlisted my help in dealing with a dilemma. Theta Chi is a national fraternity whose charter in those years was specific and discriminatory— no non-Caucasians allowed. But at the University of Minnesota, the governing body for student organizations directed Greek organizations to drop racial exclusivity. The Senate Committee on Student Affairs allowed some latitude to organizations like ours that had national charters to obey. It directed Theta Chi and the ten other

fraternities that were still segregated in 1953 (forty-nine other soror-
ities and fraternities had already integrated) to submit a report on
the chapter's progress or intended progress toward removing racial
restrictions on membership.

The student president, Bob Engstrom, asked me for advice. I was
the president of the local chapter's alumni corporation. Bob sent
a letter saying he would like to integrate promptly. To remain one
of the dwindling number of fraternities that was segregated would
result in adverse publicity for Theta Chi, he argued.

I agreed. I also thought integrating the chapter was the right
thing to do.

I sent a letter to the fraternity's national president, Sherwood
Blue, asking for clarification of the national organization's attitude
about integrated chapters and any advice he cared to share. What
ensued was a spirited exchange of correspondence over several
months in which I sought some sign of flexibility in the national
organization's enforcement of its race rule, while those at the New
Jersey headquarters insisted that fraternities were private organizations whose membership rules ought not be altered because of
external pressure.

The episode was a small skirmish in a long national struggle
to extend all of the benefits of higher education to all Americans,
regardless of color or background. It didn't last long enough to produce a dramatic result, at least not right away. But it reminds me
that the twentieth-century crusade for racial justice was a mass
movement in which a lot of people in a lot of places had roles to
play in creating change. That's what citizenship is about.

SAD NEWS CAME IN 1979. My brother Jerry, one of twin brothers
five years my junior, died by his own hand at his home in a suburb
of Oakland, California. He had worked for most of his adult life for
the Ford Motor Co. He had never married and had no children.

A suicide is always hard for the survivors to accept. I asked many
questions of those who were closer to him than I had been in his
last years. Finally his twin, our brother Joe, said, "Tom, did you
know Jerry was gay?"

I'm sad to say that I did not. I wasn't close enough to him to have discerned even something so fundamental in his nature, and I regret that he didn't feel willing or able to tell me about his orientation himself. I'm sad, too, because if he couldn't tell me, he likely was also keeping his nature a secret from many more people who cared about him. I'll never know precisely why he chose not to be openly gay or exactly how that figured in his suicide. I'll never know what I might have done to help him. But I know that attitudes about homosexuality in the United States during his lifetime were not healthy and needed to change.

Not long after Jerry died, I was serving on the board of Working Opportunities for Women, an organization helping women make the transition from homemaker to employee. Its executive director asked me for a private conversation.

"I'm a lesbian," she announced. "And the chair of our board doesn't like it."

I assured her that her orientation made no difference to me and no difference to the work of the organization. I urged her to stay. But she did not remain long. I think the board chair's attitude pushed her away. That kind of thing was all too common and was a waste of human capital.

In later years, when gay rights activists would come to the State Capitol, I would occasionally come too. I was at the rally on the Capitol steps in 2006 in protest of state Sen. Michele Bachmann's attempt to use the state constitution to ban same-sex marriage. Bachmann, who went on to Tea Party leadership in Congress, made that rally memorable by being spotted hiding in some Capitol bushes to watch the proceedings. Bachmann's amendment finally went on the state ballot in 2012, only to be rejected by the state's voters. The campaign to defeat the amendment was robust enough to push legalization of same-sex marriage through the Legislature in 2013. It's a change I am glad to see.

CHAPTER 31

Millie's Ashes

I ALWAYS ADMIRED ARLENE'S OLDEST SISTER, Mildred Jeffrey. Arlene, the youngest of the McWilliams sisters, sometimes faulted Millie for insufficient attention to the McWilliams family. That criticism may have been warranted, but Millie had an excuse. She was busy reforming the world. She spent her whole life working for social and economic justice for disadvantaged and working people. As a student at the University of Minnesota in the 1920s—long before such things were in vogue—she was involved with the Women's International League for Peace and Freedom and the YWCA hosting interracial dances and trying to racially integrate local restaurants. She spent most of her career in Detroit as a leader in the United Auto Workers, the women's movement, and the Democratic Party; she was also a sixteen-year member and one-term chair of the Wayne State University Board of Governors. Many people credit her for Walter Mondale's selection of Geraldine Ferraro as his 1984 running mate, giving the nation its first female major-party vice presidential candidate. When she died in 2004, her passing made national headlines.

Arlene and I and daughter Barbara attended a memorial service in Detroit, a big affair at which Gov. Jennifer Granholm and U.S. Sen. Debbie Stabenow spoke. We connected there with Millie's two children, son Balfour, a professor at the University of Montana in Missoula, and daughter Sharon, married to a jewelry designer and living in San Rafael, California. Given their locations, Arlene offered to take care of the cost and arrangements for Mildred's ashes, which were to be buried in the McWilliams family plot in Marcus, Iowa. As next of kin, Sharon had possession of her mother's ashes and told Arlene she would ship them to us right after she returned to California.

Shortly after we came home from Detroit, my brother Joe's wife Lucy and daughter Leslie, who live in California, came to Minnesota and spent a few days with us. Some days after they left, a package arrived from California. We assumed it was from Millie's daughter Sharon and didn't bother opening it. We just sent it on to Marcus, Iowa, where the cemetery was expecting Mildred's ashes to arrive via such a shipment.

A few days later, Lucy called to ask whether we'd received her thank-you gift. It was a tablecloth, Lucy said. "No," Arlene replied. Lucy said she would send another, which she did. It arrived a few days later.

On the same day we got the tablecloth, we had a call from the manager of the cemetery in Marcus. "What am I supposed to do with the tablecloth?" he asked.

That question triggered one of the worst days of my life. Our assumption that the first package from California contained Mildred's ashes was clearly in error. We had two tablecloths—or would, when we retrieved the first one from Iowa—and no ashes. But the ashes should have arrived days earlier. Had they been delivered to us and set aside during the hubbub of hosting my relatives? Had a careless delivery person left them outside the house? Could it be that we had lost the remains of Arlene's most famous relative? We looked and looked, then decided to face the music and call Arlene's niece Sharon.

"Oh, gee, I forgot to mail them," she said almost casually. I wonder whether she could detect our relief as we heard those words. It took a few days more, but we eventually got Mildred to Iowa and our tablecloth to Minnesota.

CHAPTER 32

All in the Family

AFTER THIRTY-THREE YEARS, Arlene and I consider Lilydale home. But for our four children, the Swain family home will always be the three-story house on Riverwood Place in St. Paul where they grew up. We left that house for Stillwater in 1971 because Arlene insisted, "We are not going to spend our old age in a three-story house." Grown though they were, Jo Anne, Barbara, and Mary protested the decision. They thought we'd taken away their birthright. Jo Anne, who was teaching in St. Paul in 1971, and Mary, then a senior at the University of Minnesota, went to the airport to pick up Barbara as she came home for winter break from her social work master's degree program at Case Western University. They wanted to be the ones to break to her the tragic news that Arlene and I were abandoning their St. Paul home.

Son Tom was still living with us, but the move didn't mean a change in schools for him. He was a senior at St. Paul Academy the year we moved—the only one of our children educated there. The girls were all products of Our Lady of Peace High School in St. Paul, which was on the site now occupied by William Mitchell College of Law.

We decided that Spike and I could commute to St. Paul together in the mornings, and he could take the bus or we could drive home together at night. That gave us some conversation time that I enjoyed. It also made him witness to my driving skill on an icy day when a car came toward us down a hill, spinning out of control. I headed for the ditch. The spinning car contained students from Stillwater High School and a young driver who didn't fully appreciate the caution that icy roads required.

We were sold on St. Paul Academy for Spike because of its reputation for maximizing academic performances. They taught Spike how to manage his time, organize his work, and study effectively. He graduated on the B honor roll, plus was all-conference in football and captain of the hockey team that went to the state tournament. His closest friends today are some of his St. Paul Academy classmates.

It was there that he met Laura Cummins, the love of his life. They started college separately, Tom in Willamette, Oregon, and Laura in Denver, but after one year they got together at the University of Oregon. They've been together ever since. Though he's our youngest, he was the second of our children to marry, after Jo Anne and Pat Murray. Tom went on to a fine career at the Toro Co., where today he's president of MTI Distributing, a Toro subsidiary. He and Laura have three children, Andrew, whom we call Drew, and twins Patrick and Merritt. Drew and his wife Andrea just had their first child, Fitzgerald; Drew works at Thompson Reuters. Patrick and Merritt are both college graduates working in the Twin Cities.

NOTHING MAKES ME FEEL OLD like the realization that three of my four children are old enough to be on Medicare and the fourth, son Tom, isn't far behind. But what a blessing it has been to have all four of them and their spouses living nearby in Minnesota! They've given us seven grandchildren and, to date, four great-grandchildren. Though the next generations are scattered geographically, they are a big part of our lives.

Daughter Jo Anne emerged from the trauma of Patrick Murray's death to become an educator specializing in English language learning (ELL) and had a thirty-five-year career in St. Paul schools. Her husband, Edward Driscoll, is a former president of the Larkin Hoffman law firm and former chairman of the state Commerce Commission during the term of DFL Gov. Wendell Anderson. Jo Anne helped raise Ed's four children and finished her career as an ELL consultant to suburban school districts. She and Ed live in Mendota Heights.

Barbara's career has been in social work, with employment first at Family and Children's Services in Minneapolis, then at the Bloomington school district, where she works today. Sadly, she lost her husband of twenty-seven years, Dennis Johnson, to a bicycling accident in Colorado in 2011. Johnson was a personal injury attorney at Meshbesher and Spence in Minneapolis and had been an Army paratrooper during the Vietnam War. Barbara and Dennis had one child, Lisa, who lives in the Seattle area and works for a nonprofit organization.

Mary turned down our offer to pay for a few years of college out-of-state and stayed loyal to the University of Minnesota, where she graduated in 1972. She worked in business for several years and married Steven Goldstein in a small ceremony on the deck of our Stillwater home. Steve had an exceptional career, including executive positions at WCCO Radio, Colfax Broadcasting, and the University of Minnesota Foundation. They have three children, McWilliam—he goes by Will, though I call him Mac—Andrea, and Thomas Nicholas, who goes by Nick. I call him Tom Nick. One shouldn't waste a good name like Tom. Will and his wife, Jessica, live in Cleveland, where she is finishing her residency in pediatric neurology and he is caring for their two children; Andrea is with Target Corp. and married to Chad Myeroff, an orthopedic surgery resident at the University of Minnesota; and Nick, employed at Accenture, and his wife, Katie, have one child, Steve, and another on the way.

SOME FRIENDS ARE SO DEAR that they become family. That's how we felt about Bill and Margaret Hruza. Residents of Madelia, Minnesota, in the 1950s and 1960s may remember Bill as their local doctor. We knew the Hruzas as our across-the-street neighbors on Logan Avenue in Minneapolis in the late 1940s and early 1950s, sharing the adventures of starting our families. Two of our daughters were born within days of two of theirs. They were natives of Montana and childhood sweethearts. Bill received his medical training at the University of Minnesota, then served as a Navy physician during some of the worst battles of World War II, on Saipan, Tinian, and Iwo Jima. He was one of only four men in his forty-two-member medical crew left standing at noon of the first day of the Iwo Jima invasion. Though they didn't stay in Minneapolis long, we became lifelong friends and occasional vacation companions. They retired to their beloved Montana in 1985; Bill died about ten years later, and Margaret died in 2014.

I credit Bill with helping me over a rough patch with Arlene. Our two-bedroom house on Logan Avenue had an unfinished second story. As our family grew, I decided to finish it as bedrooms for our daughters, doing most of the work myself on nights and weekends. It was a slow process. Late one night, I swung a hammer at a nail, missed, and hit my left forefinger—hard.

I went downstairs seeking sympathy from Arlene for my throbbing finger. Instead, she said, "I don't know how much more of this I can stand."

I erupted. How much she could stand was not my biggest concern just then.

Dr. Hruza arrived. He examined my injury, then drilled a hole in my fingernail to allow for release of some of the blood pooling under it. The throbbing eased, and so did the spousal irritation on our side of Logan Avenue.

WHEN I TURNED EIGHTY, I was called upon to say a few words at a public event about longevity. Growing old is a privilege denied to many. I attributed my long life to good genes, Minnesota's wholesomeness, the love of my four children and seven grandchildren— and Arlene.

"Few would describe our union as serene, tranquil, or idyllic," I allowed that day, with Arlene on hand. "'Spirited' is a more apt description." The week before, daughter Barbara and her family had sent us an anniversary card with a message that seemed fitting: "Mom and Dad—still driving each other crazy after all these years."

"Notwithstanding," I added, our marriage "has worked, nurtured, and lasted. Arlene occasionally, sometimes frequently, suggests I count my blessings, claiming it is doubtful any other woman would have put up with me this long. It's probably true. But it is definitely true that with her care, support, and love, we have enjoyed good health and success."

The last chapter of Arlene's life was spent at a care facility next door to my apartment near our home in Lilydale. Vascular dementia and several strokes took a progressive and irreversible toll. Yet during our daily visits, Arlene's old spark occasionally reappeared. I was delighted when she volunteered one day, "I wish we still lived together so I could keep telling you what not to do." The inevitable end came on February 24, 2015. I was at her side—and she will always be at mine.

CHAPTER 33

On Leadership

I'VE MOSTLY BEEN A NUMBER-TWO PERSON—a team player, facilitator, implementer, organizer, get-it-done guy supporting the superb bosses for whom I've worked. They were among Minnesota's best—Peter Popovich, Elmer Andersen, Ron Hubbs, Carl Drake, Nils Hasselmo, Mark Yudof, Bob Bruininks. I was a good fit for a secondary role. I'm not a dominant personality or a charismatic figure. I've made myself available, and opportunities to be of service have come my way.

I'm keen on seeking consensus. That's an essential skill for effective participation in democracy. When one cares about a cause, one ought to work to build support for it. That's better done if others can trust you to be fair, to listen, to respect their views, and to be willing to compromise. Those are attributes worth cultivating.

I've long admired the ideas expressed in the prose poem "Desiderata," written in 1927 by Max Ehrmann. Its title is Latin for "desired things." It comes close to expressing my leadership credo: "Without surrender be on good terms with all persons. Speak your truth quietly and clearly; and listen to others, even the dull and the ignorant; they too have their story."

Being on good terms with others does not mean being subservient, however. Patricia Johnson, who succeeded me as CEO at State Fund Mutual Insurance Co., wrote some kind words about me in connection with the Women Who Appreciate Tom Swain luncheon in August 1994. She observed that I'm not uncomfortable around people who are assertive in voicing their ideas or who may be smarter than me. "He is attracted to the good idea, never mind the source," she said. I liked that, and I hope it's true.

Americans tend to focus on the individual—individual rights, individual responsibilities, individual leadership. We would do well to see that the leadership America needs also arises from collective activity. Being a good steward of organizations that provide leadership is important and rewarding civic work.

I consider the University of Minnesota the most critically important institution in the state. Supporting it with time and treasure so that it can be a leader is among the best contributions a Minnesotan can make. I was most pleased in 2001 when, in conjunction with my eightieth birthday, a group of my friends established the Thomas H. Swain Fellowship in Public Leadership at the university's Humphrey School of Public Affairs. The idea originated with my good friend David Metzen, a former chair of the Board of Regents and a lifelong educator who was introduced to me by his South St. Paul high school classmate Jean LeVander King, Gov. Harold LeVander's daughter and a leader in her own right. Dave saw that lack of funding is a major impediment to midcareer professionals who would benefit from additional graduate education. That funding, $10,000 for a year of study, is what the Swain Fellowship provides. Initially we could afford two Swain Fellows per year; now there are three.

I've come to know many of the Swain Fellows, and I'm very proud of them. Just a few of them are Elizabeth Glidden, now vice chair of the Minneapolis City Council; state Rep. Jim Davnie of Minneapolis; Minneapolis Park Board member Tracy Nordstrom; and Laura Williams, a program manager at the Sexual Violence Justice Institute. I've recently come to know Tracy Moore, a Minneapolis Fire Department captain who used the Swain Fellowship stipend to get a master's degree in public affairs. One of the papers she did in her master's work was about discrimination against women in the fire department—a persistent problem, perhaps more acute in that line of work than in most others. Tracy's goal in getting a master's degree is to prepare herself for a leadership role in the fire department, helping it promote change and improve the morale of all employees. She has also worked with the Somali population to help them better understand the services that her department provides, an effort that brought the Minneapolis Fire Department notice and acclaim. As a sideline, Tracy and her spouse Renee have a business helping older people like me who are downsizing to sell their unwanted goods on the Internet. Having my name on a program that gives a boost to people like Tracy is a real thrill for me.

I've been involved in many other fine Minnesota organizations that have been leaders in what they do. There's nothing in other states like the Citizens League, which I served as president in 1985–86. For three generations, it's been the place where citizens can leave their partisan hatchets at the door and confront this state's thorniest problems together. Through the years, Citizens League study commissions have been a source of impressive new solutions to public problems—things like how to keep school quality up even in property-poor places and how to build a metropolitan area where prosperity is widely shared. I hope the league can step up its idea-generating work.

Another unique homegrown organization that does great work is Twin Cities RISE! I've served on its board for more than ten years. Its founder, former General Mills executive Steve Rothschild, is one of my heroes. He left the corporate world because he had an idea that unemployed adults, primarily black men, could and should be mentored and trained for the jobs that Twin Cities employers have trouble filling. The Twin Cities RISE! approach involves one-on-one coaching and education, including internships, and its unique Personal Empowerment program enables participants to transform their lives. Graduates of the RISE! program move into jobs with average starting salaries of more than $25,000 and a retention rate after one year of more than 80 percent. It's the best approach I've seen for pulling young people out of poverty.

Courage Center, where I was a board member for ten years and board chair from 1992 to 1994, ranks among the nation's best providers of services to physically disabled and sensory-impaired people. It recently merged with the Sister Kenny organization to become Courage Kenny Rehabilitation Center. It does a superb job helping those with physical challenges accept their situation with courage and a positive outlook while showing them how to make the most of the abilities they still have.

I'm proud of Common Bond Communities, on whose board I also served. It's a nationally recognized pioneer in transforming the lives of the homeless poor. It provides both low-cost housing and an array of services to address the physical, mental, and social ills of those housed in its units. Based in St. Paul, it now serves over fifty communities in three states and was among the first organizations of its kind to recognize that its mix of housing and services is needed in the suburbs as well as the inner city. When the David W. Preus Leadership Award in 1997 allowed me to designate a charity to receive the award's $1,000 prize, I chose Common Bond.

Some of the most rewarding work I've done was begun when I was past age seventy. Take the Minnesota Health Care Commission, which I chaired for three years beginning in 1992, at age seventy-one. That year, I told a reporter for *City Business* newspaper that I was aware of the high risk of failure in any effort to reform an industry as complex and inbred as health care. But senior citizens are uniquely positioned to take such risks. They no longer have to fret about what failure might mean for their long-term career aspirations. "Every assignment you take as you get older shouldn't be those that are safe," I said. "Keep testing yourself." You're never too old to take risks.

I'm taking one right now. I'm cochair of the Friends of the St. Paul Libraries' capital campaign. We aim to raise $7.8 million in private funds to support major renovations at two branch libraries, Sun Ray and Highland Park, and some modest improvements at the downtown library, recently named for my friend, former St. Paul Mayor George Latimer. I've always been proud of the quality of St. Paul's public libraries. The money we're raising is going to help improve libraries' service to families with young children, making them important centers for early learning.

People are living longer today, but the U.S. retirement age hasn't changed much—yet. That may be coming. Today a whole industry has developed around counseling retirees about managing their money and their health. There should also be emphasis on helping retirees see the options they have for constructive use of their time. My motto is, "It's better to wear out than to rust out." Opportunities came rather easily to me because I had already been active in public affairs. I've seen others, able people, who don't have a clue how they can contribute to the community in retirement. Preretirement counseling ought to include some coaching about ways to make oneself available for community service—and community organizations ought to be reaching out to new retirees.

I'm disappointed when I hear about business and professional leaders retreating at the end of the workday to gated neighborhoods and leaving the problems of the rest of society to someone else. That's not how the leaders I admired lived. Granted, the time pressure on today's two-earner families is greater than it was when most families had only one breadwinner. But civic organizations that have been important to Minnesota's quality of life have declined, and we will all pay a price if that trend continues. Somehow we as a society have to find ways to do the work that voluntary associations have always done in this state, even though the majority of adults between the ages of twenty-five and sixty-five are employed. Employers too have a role to play. Their demands ought not be so excessive that they deprive workers of the chance to be good citizens, responsible for their families and their communities.

Being involved in public and social service activities has been energizing and rewarding for me. My life has been richer as a result. I hope I've also contributed something of value to others.

Chronology

Tom Swain has received many awards for his work, most notably the 2004 National Governors Association award for public service by a private citizen; he was one of only three in the nation so honored that year. Here is a summary of his many professional accomplishments, activities, and recognitions.

Employment History

Junior public accountant, Lybrand, Ross Bros., and Montgomery, Rockford, Illinois, 1942–43

Airman, U.S. Army Air Corps, 1943–46

Athletic scholastic advisor, University of Minnesota Athletic Department, 1946–47

Administrative assistant, State of Minnesota, Department of Aeronautics, 1947–48

Athletic ticket manager, University of Minnesota, 1948–51

Manager, Convention and Visitors Bureau, St. Paul Chamber of Commerce, 1951–56

Executive director, Minnesota Statehood Centennial Commission, State of Minnesota, 1956–59

Executive director, Minnesota Insurance Information Center, 1959–60

Campaign manager, Elmer L. Andersen for Governor, State of Minnesota, 1960

Chief of staff, Gov. Elmer L. Andersen, State of Minnesota, 1961

Commissioner, Department of Business Development, State of Minnesota, 1961–62

Director on behalf of Governor Andersen, 1962 election recount effort, 1962–63

The St. Paul Companies, 1963–86 (retired as executive vice president)

CEO, State Fund Mutual Insurance Company, 1992

Interim vice president of Institutional Relations, University of Minnesota, 1996–98

Interim vice president of University Relations, University of Minnesota, 2004

Civic and Philanthropic Activities

Health

St. Paul Children's Hospital Board of Directors, 1977–82

Minnesota Coalition–Low Birth Rate (Life at Any Price), 1984–85

Select Care Board of Directors, 1990–95

Chair, Minnesota Health Care Commission, 1992–95

Minnesota Forum on Health Care Costs, 2003–4

Trustee, Associated Capital Hospitals

Minnesota Coalition on Health

Minnesota Center for Bio-Medical Ethics

State of Minnesota

Minnesota Lawyers Professional Responsibility Board, 1981–87

Minnesota News Council, 1987–92

State of Minnesota Compensation Council, 1987–2012 (chair)

University of Minnesota Regent Candidate Advisory Council, 1988–94 (vice chair)

Commission on Judicial Selection, 1989–2008

Judicial Performance Evaluation Study Committee, 2008–9

Governor's Commission on Sports

Chair, Fort Snelling Sesquicentennial Planning Committee

University of Minnesota

University of Minnesota Foundation, twenty years, now life trustee

Hubert H. Humphrey School of Public Affairs Advisory Committee, since 2003

Intercollegiate Athletics Advisory Committee, 2000–2012

Director, Osher Life Long Learning Board, 1995–2008 (president, 1998–2000)

All U Honors Committee, 1983–85, 2006–7

Board member, University of Minnesota Alumni Association, 1970–78 (national president, 1976–77)

City of St. Paul

Chair, Chamber of Commerce Public Conduct and Concern Committee, 1969–93

Landmarks Board of Directors, 1980–85

Chair of committee to develop DARE program in all St. Paul schools for fifth grade, 1988–92

Mayor's Task Force on Police Priorities, 1991–92

Friends of St. Paul Public Library Board of Directors, 2002–11

Cochair, Friends of St. Paul Public Library capital campaigns, 1998–2000, 2012–14

Chamber of Commerce Higher Education Task Force

St. Paul Arts and Science Council Board of Directors

St. Paul Chamber of Commerce Solicitation Control Subcommittee

Depot Concourse Task Force

Social Services

Courage Center Board of Directors, 1986–96 (chair, 1992–94)

United Arts Council Board of Directors, 1988–89

Common Bond Communities Board, 1994–2000

Twin Cities RISE! Board of Directors, since 2000

Schubert Club Board of Directors
    Chair, Schubert Club 125th Anniversary Campaign

Working Opportunities for Women Board

Minnesota State Council on Economic Education Board

Spring Hill Center Board

Minnesota Newspaper Foundation Board

Consultant, Management Assistant Program (clients included Prevention Alliance, Arlington House, Good Neighbor Foundation, House of Charity)

American for Generational Equality, Minnesota Chapter

Catholic Charities of St. Paul Board of Directors

Twin Cities International Program Board of Directors

International Institute of St. Paul Board of Directors

Indianhead Council Boy Scouts of America Board of Directors

National Retiree Volunteer Coalition Board of Directors

Civic

Cochair of campaign to make City of St. Paul an independent school district, 1964

Citizens League of the Twin Cities Board, 1979–92 (president, 1985–86)

Chair, Real Estate Development Committee, Citizens League of the Twin Cities Board, 1984–85

Chair, Operations Committee, Citizens League of the Twin Cities Board, 1981–82

Chair, City of Lilydale Planning Commission, 1997–2006 (member since 2011)

Mayor, City of Lilydale, 2007–10

Politics

Republican State Executive Committee, 1960s

Republican State Central Committee

Republican Fourth District Executive Committee

Chair, Republican Fourth District Rules Committee

Chair, Republican Fourth District Resolution Committee

Index

TOM H. SWAIN has made notable contributions to Minnesota higher education, politics, corporate affairs, and health care for more than six decades. He served as chief of staff to former Minnesota Governor Elmer L. Andersen and was an executive with The St. Paul Companies, State Fund Mutual Insurance Co., and the University of Minnesota. He has received numerous local and national awards, including an honorary doctor of laws degree from the University of Minnesota, an award from the National Governors Association, and an Outstanding Achievement Award from the University of Minnesota.

LORI STURDEVANT is an editorial writer and columnist for the *Star Tribune* of Minneapolis–St. Paul. Her books include *Her Honor: Rosalie Wahl and the Minnesota Women's Movement*, *The Pillsburys of Minnesota*, and *A Man's Reach*, written with former Minnesota governor Elmer L. Andersen (Minnesota, 2000).